ADVANCE PRAISE FOR
UNRAVELING AMBITION

"So inspiring! With humor and heart, Valia helps readers understand the roots of their ambition so they can confidently design a purpose-driven life. *Unraveling Ambition* is a timely and indispensable companion for both emerging and established leaders in the post-pandemic era."

— Robert Chatwani, President, *Docusign*

"Beautiful and brilliant. Jump in and you'll soon find yourself asking, 'Isn't that how we *all* want to live our lives?' Valia provides us with the exact moment to explore the question with purpose, peace, and pause. *Unraveling Ambition* will grab you from chapter one with an invitation that feels like a soothing and mesmerizing calling. We are all ready for this work and just needed this guidance—beautifully handed to us here."

— Lisa Dallenbach, Chief People Officer, *theSkimm*

"Ambition is so revered, it's rarely questioned. Valia takes it head on, using her own story in an authentic, effective provocation. Laying bare the false choices and inevitable consequences, she pivots—how do we resolve this tension? If you want to channel your ambition towards greater purpose and impact, she is a resonant, credible, and reassuring voice."

— Marty Coyne, Founder & Principal, *Matchstick*, Inventor

"I sighed deeply many times as I recognized myself—the good, the bad, the past, the future—in the pages of *Unraveling Ambition*. Valia's writing made me laugh, moved me to tears and made me think more clearly about the importance of balance and intentionality in leadership. She has turned the wisdom gained from her own personal journey into practical and tangible thoughts and actions that propel her readers more purposefully on their own journeys as leaders and as humans."

— Brooke Gordon, Partner & Co-Chief Operating Officer North America, *FGS Global*

"*Unraveling Ambition* is more than a book on leadership. Valia has the voice of raw truth and love—she is 'whisperer' to us as we continue on our quest to find deeper fulfillment, make real connections with ourselves and others, and uncover true joy."

— Connie Kim, Head of Learning & Development and Diversity, Equity, Inclusion & Belonging, *Heineken USA*

"Valia provides a refreshing and empowering perspective on leadership and ambition that challenges readers to rethink their approach to personal development. *Unraveling Ambition* offers practical insights and is an authentic guide to claiming personal power."

— Archana Agrawal, Chief Marketing Officer, *Airtable*

"*Unraveling Ambition* has put, in text form, ideas and concepts that Valia has imparted to me that have changed my life. For years, I've tried to figure out how to best describe Valia. My career coach. . . my life coach. . . my spiritual guide. I'm grateful the world finally gets to enjoy *Unraveling Ambition*—leaders everywhere just got the answers to 'unlocking' the test."

— Kyle Mosley, Media Executive

"Valia creates a beautiful space for her reader to engage with deep issues under her guidance. There is something so trustworthy and down-to-earth erudite about how Valia writes. The book is authentic, full of wisdom, funny, natural, kind—and with a very clear message of claiming personal power."

– Irini Kalamakis, Senior Managing Director & Global Head of Strategic Partnerships, *Omers*

"If you are ready to begin your own journey of unraveling—or know someone who needs a nudge—this is the manual. I have personally and repeatedly witnessed Valia's process transform lives and am amazed that her writing creates the feeling of listening. Valia has been a ballast in my life. She embodies leading by example. At the outset of a new engagement, she leads by immediately creating a safe space for vulnerability by sharing a personal story. You cannot ask of your team that of which you are not willing to do yourself. Her insides unquestionably match her outsides and I am thrilled that her gifts will now be able to be shared with a wider audience."

– Crescent Muhammad, Managing Director, *Council of Urban Professionals*

"Like a long hug from an old friend, I immediately felt connection, comfort, and clarity while reading *Unraveling Ambition*. As a lifelong 'good girl' myself, I have often felt that my purpose in life was to please and be in service to others. Through Valia's lighthearted and vulnerable storytelling, I was able to see that it's okay to allow that version of myself to unravel, to expose, in order to allow a more aligned and powerful version to emerge."

– Kacey Taormina, Residential & Commercial Real Estate Broker, Bravo TV Star, Entrepreneur

"Whether you are an accomplished executive or a forest-bound seeker, stop a moment to take this vista in. In a sea of self-help, leadership, and coaching books, Valia manages to achieve that rarest of accomplishments—a book that is part inspirational inner prayer and part conspiratorial conversation into the wee hours with the most intimate of friends. Valia destroys our distracting distinctions of personal and professional and demands that we define for ourselves once and for all who we are. *Unraveling Ambition* will convince you that you need no book to find yourself and that your ease, your energy and your rhythm is already inside. Valia will help you stand for your Self. . . and not only win, but realize you've been winning all along."

— Matthew Kwatinetz, Director, *NYU Urban Lab* and Senior Real Estate Executive, Film Producer

"As someone who has worked with Valia for well over a decade, let me tell you—*Unraveling Ambition* is a gift. It authentically channels everything we all need to hear right now in order to challenge the assumptions and actions we're actually trapping ourselves with. Buy this book for yourself and devour it as I did. You'll never stop thanking yourself. Then buy this book for everyone you know. You'll be making the world a better place."

— Kate Vanek, Global COO & CFO, *True Platform*

UNRAVELING
AMBITION

LIVING AND LEADING FROM THE INSIDE-OUT

VALIA GLYTSIS

Publishing support provided by
Ignite Press
5070 N. Sixth St. #189
Fresno, CA 93710
www.IgnitePress.us

ISBN: 979-8-9884152-0-6
ISBN: 979-8-9884152-1-3 (Hardcover)
ISBN: 979-8-9884152-2-0 (E-book)

For bulk purchases and for booking, contact:

Valia Glytsis
valia@leadwithvalia.com
www.leadwithvalia.com

Library of Congress Control Number: 2023909066

Cover design by Klassic Designs
Edited by Elizabeth Arterberry
Interior design by Jetlaunch

FIRST EDITION

For Yiayia and her endless expanses of love.

ACKNOWLEDGMENTS

On this journey of unraveling ambition, I learned that gratitude is the antidote to fear. Fear has poked its nefarious head onto my path more times than I can count. Fear of loss, fear of abandonment, fear of mediocrity. It prevented my progress and stifled my self-expression.

Gratitude has been a torch of comfort. It has allowed me to unclench from fear's grip and lean into the good that surrounds us all. It has cracked open a window through which love can pour in. I've also learned that gratitude magnifies when it is made explicit.

• • •

To my parents: Thank you for always believing in me, my voice, and my gifts. The choices you made have allowed me to live a truly blessed life as a first-generation Greek American. So many of the stories in this book illustrate the complications of carrying your deep desires for my success. While my many years of blind ambition were trying, I never forget your boundless love, support, and cheerleading.

Mammie, thank you for showing me what it means to love as only a mother can. You have never questioned a single one of my hopes, dreams, and ambitions. You have always been there for every mundane and meaningful moment of my life and because of you I know what it means to be loved so hard.

Babbie, thank you for knowing there was an author in me even before I knew how to write. You have always pushed for my excellence—in finances, education, career—and provided me the path to achieve that excellence. You have taught me your love for experiencing the world and its people, a true anthropologist.

Irini, there is no sister with whom I'd rather co-travel this life than you. Thank you for being my witness, my champion, my very best friend. Few are blessed to have the connection we share. As we grow older and see how rare true friendship is, I bow down to the Universe for bringing us together so serendipitously forty years ago.

To my daughter, Emilia: You have expanded my life, my joy, and my heart in unimaginable ways. Our mother-daughter journey has just begun and I thank God every day that you have chosen me as your mama. I can't wait to see what you're going to teach me in this life.

Above all, to my love, KB: Thank you for being my soul partner on this life journey of learning and unlearning. I choose you every moment of every day. I am so proud of you, and who we are becoming, together. The unraveling continues to expand, exposing new depths of our love and life. Without you, there is no story to tell.

• • •

There are so many teachers, healers, and guides who have helped me and inspired me on my spiritual leadership path. I stand on their shoulders as I write this book. My deepest gratitude to Nicole, Sarah, Alizabeth, Anne-Marie, Steve, Aimee, Piper, Cindy, and Jennifer.

To the Paradox family—my lifelong exploration of the paradox would be impossible without your unending dedication, loyalty, and love of what we do together every day. Working with each of you is an endless blessing of shared wisdom and community.

To my Editorial Board—Jena, Cathy, Irini, Karen, Nikhil, and the team at Ignite Press—thank you for holding this book so tenderly and investing your time and wisdom to help me birth it into reality.

• • •

Lastly, to my younger self. I am so proud of you. I love you.

Perfectly Imperfect

by Valia Glytsis

It hurts when I stumble
Committed to growth yet
Something so simple – a labyrinth.

Saying no, a boundary.
My insides churn feeling
The anticipation of the break.

What is abandonment
If not the loss of self.
Serving endlessly, a high enough cost.

Instead I withdraw. I please.
The safety of comfort.
Sometimes so sweet compared to growth.

Will they go away?
Or will I push them away
Quietly – like countless others.

Each in our own universe of reality.
Puppets in one another's show.
Yet ultimately inseparable as one – a cosmic joke.

To love myself allows
Another to meet me there.
To free our bond of shoulds.

I welcome the attempts.
I will try, try again.
To love, so simple. Yet perfectly imperfect.

TABLE OF CONTENTS

INTRODUCTION:
TO MY FELLOW TRAVELER

I'm so glad you're here. I don't believe in coincidences, so I will trust deeply that our meeting is divinely timed and that you are meant to receive the words on the pages that lie ahead. My hope for you is that while I share pieces of my journey, it will feel like a much-needed rest stop in your life right now. I intend for it to give you the space and tools to reflect on where you are—both personally and professionally—and assess how you might activate even more peace, power, and purpose in your every day. So, get comfortable, drop your shoulders an inch, grab a journal and a cup of tea, and settle in.

My intuitive sense is that you're tired. Perhaps not physically tired (although, who are we kidding, naps are always welcomed!), but certainly existentially tired. This is not an insult, but an invitation. I promise. I believe you have spent years searching, striving, and succeeding. You have checked all of the boxes, done all the "right" things, perhaps gathered accolades or degrees, climbed the metaphorical mountains in your life and career, worked on yourself and your relationships, and pushed for excellence in the big and tiny moments of life. How could you *not* be tired?!

However, I'd also wager that, despite all of the seeming success, something is missing. Something isn't quite right, given all of the years and effort that were poured into *making* it right. You have objectively figured most of it out, yet you aren't feeling quite on track and fully aligned with your purpose. Maybe it manifests as dreading Mondays or a mysterious slew of annoying health concerns. Perhaps you are avoiding friends and family as you desperately try to figure out your boundaries. Maybe you're in a distracted state of mind that has you multitasking and juggling aimlessly, with frustrating results. It might look like wanting to start something—a project, a new job, a company, a move—yet realizing there are zero energy reserves to initiate the process, so you keep waiting for the right moment to arrive. Basically, in the purest sense, your insides don't match your outsides, and while you can keep chugging along this way, you're wondering if there is another way. You know that there's something more baked inside of you that you need to access and unlock. You know that this isn't where the chapter ends, but that you are about to start a whole new book. As the author of the story, perhaps?

A little about me so we can get better acquainted. I don't see all of these things in *you* without full awareness that the mirror reflects right back at *me*. I am inviting you into this space of truth-telling because I need it, too. Desperately, in fact. Our lives are too precious to live another repetitive season without zooming out to do some inventory and assess. What's the current state? What's working and what's not? What's the future state? Why does this matter anyway? And how on earth do we build a bridge between the present and the future? It's time to fully align our minds with our hearts and with our spirits. Only then can we sync our insides with our outsides and find the peace and harmony we so secretly crave. I believe that this is what the imminent genre of spiritual leadership is all about, and I feel humbled to be a participant in its genesis. Spiritual leadership is about living with intentionality—building a life integrated with our full presence, curiosity, and trust.

I make sense of the world through writing. I believe the written word is like a sacred portal, a gateway. It helps me trade understanding for trust. It allows me to translate a feeling so enormous into a concept that we can unpack and explore together. I was very intentional about choosing the word "unraveling" as the first one you would read on the cover. I believe that the process of unraveling something is sacred, and, while existentially reflective in nature, it is also highly practical and relevant to our daily reality.

> Spiritual leadership is about living with intentionality.

When I was interviewing publishers, one of them said to me: "You probably want to lose the word 'unraveling.' It doesn't sound positive or optimistic and the reader might think they need to do a lot of work."

I laughed out loud, politely suggested that we are probably not the right fit, and thanked them for their time. *Spoiler alert:* Unraveling *isn't* positive or optimistic and it *is* a lot of work. Knowing what I think I know about you, you wouldn't have it any other way. We read the word "unraveling" and it reverberates in our being as a declaration of its necessity. You and I both know that, to lead the lives we were meant to live, it will require an excavation to set us free. From there, we can create our future from who we are *today*, rather than endlessly recreate our future from the holds of the past (and, unsurprisingly, keep getting the same old results).

The second word you read on this book's cover was "ambition." Ambition is my kryptonite. It has been the driving force behind so much of my life's story. In my experience, it is loaded with habits and rituals and beliefs comprised of complicated recipes with ingredients like effort, work, responsibility, and the drive to always search for more. That darn word "more" is an endless abyss of insecurity. In the anthology of stories to follow, you'll learn quite a bit about my ambition and how it's both served and haunted me throughout my life's path.

I urge you to take this book as an invitation and think about what needs unraveling in your life. What is your Achilles heel? It might be ambition, it might be something related, or it might be something entirely different. Unraveling stress? Unraveling boredom? Unraveling procrastination? The word itself doesn't matter as much as the energy behind it. You'll know that you've reached the central thread that needs unraveling when you can see it weaving in and out of every aspect of your life—your choices, your relationships, even your daily routine.

I'm going to share reflections and lessons with you at very different altitudes of ambition to show you how deeply enmeshed we become in our belief systems. Some chapters focus on very literal and logical manifestations of ambition like education, career, and accolades. Other chapters will take you into deeper parts of the human experience—perhaps a strange place to meet ambition—for example, how we love, how we relate to time, how we forgive. Alongside these altitude shifts within the narrative, you'll notice the pendulum swinging between some very practical aspects of personal leadership—tips, tools, techniques to amplify your day-to-day—as well as some richer spiritual prompts for self-reflection and questioning what we hold to be true.

Warning: Altitude shifts *and* pendulum swings will catalyze a lot of movement in you. You're completely safe and on the right track, even if it feels disorienting from time to time.

What's not written on the cover of this book—though it is an important thread throughout the story and a catalyst for my launching into unraveling in the first place—is my experience as a first-generation Greek American. Not surprisingly, my cultural roots have profoundly shaped how I see the world. The push-pull of the first-generation experience is an endless loop of ancestry versus reinvention, tradition versus progress, community versus individuality, stability versus freedom—the list goes on. You live in the in-between each and every day. Every decision has weight and implications.

My "first" experience is a cultural one; yours might be different. Perhaps you're the first in your family to go to college, start a company, move to another part of the world, lead a team, leave the family business, quit a job without having another one, have children without a partner, or pursue a passion with nothing but the sheer belief that you can make a living from it. You get the point. No matter what type of "first" you are, it *takes* something to be that "first." It asks something of you. In a way, ambition is implied in or at least inferred from the shadows. *Since you're the first, do it well. Do it right. Do it best. Do it perfectly. Do it for us.*

Extracting ambition from being a "first" is an excruciating *and* critical part of unraveling. Did I mention I'm so glad you're here? Not to worry, I've comforted you with plenty of "My Big Fat Greek Wedding" humor inside—endless comic relief (often appreciated only in hindsight) is a really delightful side effect of being first.

I wrote a previous draft of this book before 2020, and the way I wrote it, ironically, was laced with ambition even as I was teaching you how to unravel it. We're always learning the lessons that are ours to master, I suppose. The chapters were overflowing with coaching tools, leadership topics, team-building ideas, and even homework to keep you busy. While a very useful book, the energy behind it was old and unchecked. You see, I wrote it to serve you and equip you with more to-dos. I wrote it to be helpful and pleasing to my audience. I wrote it to prove that I was legitimate enough of a leadership resource, someone you could count on. The ambition manifested in a head-based urge to "do it right" rather than speaking to you from the heart-based place of truth-telling and vulnerability. I said goodbye to that manuscript as an act of self-love, and I began again.

> We're always learning the lessons that are ours to master, I suppose.

While many of the same stories have found their way back into the book you're holding, I have recommitted to the project from a place of wanting to create art in the world. To date, my "art" has been my company—*The Paradox of Leadership*. The firm is a boutique leadership development collective that helps leaders and teams unlock the *inner* work of managing and leading. We help clients face their fears, redefine their values, build new and creative ways of using their influence, and unlock blockages to self and team trust. We are insatiable in supporting companies to double-down on the human side of business—and even start peeking into the place where business and spirituality intersect. The "art" of the paradox has inspired me for over a decade now. While we search endlessly *outside* of ourselves for meaning, purpose, and impact, it is all hidden *within* our personal narratives and habitual thought patterns. The key to becoming has little to do with ambition and is actually held in the one place we probably won't look—the quiet stillness within. I'll share a bit more of how Paradox came to be soon.

You'll see the word "leadership" sprinkled throughout the book since it's part of my daily landscape. I know that leadership can be a loaded word, embossed with socioeconomic and cultural implications depending on your vantage point. My lens of leadership has little to do with one's title, role, company, and other accolades. The invitation in this book is to discover the leader *within*. I've worked with hundreds of leaders and have come to know for sure that the ultimate paradox is how "inside-out" the game of leadership truly is. It's about the choices we make, the way we see the world, the willingness to sit with our fears without running away, the empathy we show to ourselves and eventually one another, and the willingness to unravel self-trust and build it back up again.

Whenever you read the word "leader" or "leadership"—know that I am speaking to you. No matter where you find yourself personally or professionally right now, leadership is for the one who is willing to look inside themselves and assess what gets to stay and what needs to go in order to live a truly self-actualized experience of this fascinating gift

> The invitation in this book is to discover the leader *within*.

called life. Some might call this journey into losing ambition and finding yourself a journey of privilege. Perhaps. It *does* require our greatest resource, time, to be allocated to slowing down, reflecting, and being willing to look beyond the hustle of the day-to-day. I don't see this as privilege, however. I see it as our ultimate responsibility to ourselves, our families, our communities, and—dare I say—the world. I see it as our *actual* work on the planet—to know ourselves as a means of shifting our collective consciousness from fear to love.

When I was first selecting a coaching specialty and starting my business, there were a lot of paths—wellness coaching, career coaching, life coaching –, any of which would have been fulfilling. However, I felt a gravitational pull to leadership development because I saw the power of the ripple effect. I knew that working with leaders of any type of unit or organization would have a profound, cascading influence on the lives of others. My sense of purpose became a numbers game—my commitment to leveling up the consciousness of the planet in my tiny corner of the world. This is not to sound grandiose. Ambition creeping in, perhaps? The choice was quite literal and practical. I thought about what might happen if a manager or leader learned how to be a bit more authentic, an ounce more generous, and a tad less afraid. He or she might show up more secure and therefore more willing to see others and where they are in their personal journeys, be better listeners and more empathetic, trust more deeply, and have enhanced communication and greater impact. The shifts were endless. . . I could see and *feel* the invisible ripple effect and it moved me.

There is a beautiful concept in Greek called *philoxenia*—translated literally to "love of the stranger." Philoxenia is the purest essence of hospitality, it is a state of mind and a way of being. It is the most courageous way to connect with another human being—it requires being open, curious, gracious, generous. What moves me about this concept is that it takes the paradox to a deeper, more profound level. It's not just the original paradox that leadership resides *within* each and every one of us (the choices we make, the way we see the world)—but more so that in doing this important work of self-actualization, we find ourselves in one another. Isn't that incredible? We find ourselves in one another. By peering into *my* heart, you can see aspects of *yourself*. By sharing myself with you, I know you even if we haven't yet met. By sharing with love and vulnerability, the space between us collapses. So as we love the foreign in each other, we reclaim pieces of ourselves along the way.

The time has arrived. I humbly invite you to begin your sacred journey of intentional unraveling. You get to hold your story at a slight distance and assess whether it is still valid, if it's time to start editing, or even time to say good-bye. You get to see whether the foundational assumptions in your life are really yours, or if they are simply borrowed and now over-due for return. You get to learn about your personal leadership and why it might be the most important thing you'll ever discover. I'll give you one clue before we begin: discomfort is usually a sign of having borrowed something that no longer belongs to you. It manifests as boredom, depletion, and general lethargy. Joy is usually a sign of alignment with who you truly are. It manifests as bright energy, hope, even effervescence. Both discomfort and joy are important points on our compass and deserve equal amounts of grace, curiosity, and attention.

> Joy is usually a sign of alignment with who you truly are.

I chose ambition as the singular thread that would unravel everything else in my story. What will yours be?

Know that you are seen, your life really matters, and you get to live in a world where your insides match your outsides.

With all my love,
Valia

1
KNOW THE RULES

I SUPPOSE THE writing was on the wall all along, but it wasn't until a series of panic attacks a little over a decade ago that I committed to fully unraveling and getting to know myself—my whole self—from the *inside out*. I'll skip to the punchline. The panic attacks came from living intensely *inversely*—from the *outside in*. I allowed the world to dictate who I should be and I moved mountains to ensure I could deliver, with five gold stars, no less. I was a seasoned "good girl" who had crafted a life of invisible rules and norms to grip onto whatever semblances of safety, control, and predictability she could.

Growing up as the only child of Greek immigrant parents, safety was a paramount concern. Ensuring safety (or rather, worrying about the lack of safety around every corner) was our love language. And control was the most direct route to secure the illusion of safety. In order to activate the control-as-safety-as-love mechanism, there were a lot of rules. I mean, a *lot* of rules. Rules on what to do, what not to do, exactly how to do it, and the ramifications of doing or not doing something.

The majority of the rules were of the "if. . . then" variety.

If you earn good grades, then you can choose a gift.

If you finish your homework, then you can watch Beverly Hills 90210. (Also, you can only watch TV on weekends, even though the show airs on Thursday nights. Welcome to the VHS struggles of the '90s.)

If you practice the piano for two hours, then you can play with your friend.

The rules also worked in reverse.

If you're not a good girl, then I will lock you up in the Babaoulo (Greek name for invisible dungeon used to terrify children).

If you don't ace this math test (while I'm hovering over your head with practice problems in queue), *then we'll move back to Greece and never return to your school friends.*

If you don't cut your hair short, then I will just do it in your sleep.

(That last one was very weird and caused nightmares and paranoia for years.)

The rules continued into adolescence and early adulthood.

If you get that scholarship, then I'll literally burst into tears with pride.

If you get the EMBA from Columbia University, then all of our sacrifices will have been worth it.

If you become a teacher, then all of our sacrifices will not have been worth it.

If you want to get involved in charity work, then you have to be rich first.

Let's not forget the rules pertaining to the all-consuming evil eye. (For those unfamiliar, Greeks live by the code of the evil eye. I dare say it's a religion in and of itself. Almost every Greek you meet will be sporting an evil eye on a necklace, earring, piece of home décor, tattoo, car charm, keychain, and many other explicit and/or discrete forms in order to pretend that we are in control. If we worry about it, it won't happen—right?)

If you don't want to be caught under the spell of that lady down the street, then don't talk about how well you're doing in school.

If you don't want your distant cousins to be jealous and have their mom cast the evil eye on you, then don't talk about that prize you won at the writing competition last week.

If you want to be liked, then always downplay your successes so you don't make them feel bad—or worse—jealous.

There was a very important set of rules around money. Money and control went hand in hand. If we were able to control our money, then our worries about money would be kept at bay.

If we have another excess phone bill (because I wanted to speak with my mother while she was back in Greece), *then I will yell and blame her for wasting money and hold onto this resentment for weeks* (read: years).

If you don't save every dollar you earn, then you will disappoint me and prove you are not responsible. (In later years, this softened to a daily mantra of "Hello. How are you? Don't forget to save 20%+ of what you earn.")

If you purchase an expensive gift for me, then I will immediately tell you that it was inappropriate and "too much" rather than show gratitude and appreciation.

Of course, there were also a whole set of rules around love. Love was complicated as a Greek immigrant kid. I was showered with and suffocated by it all at once.

If I really love you, I must free you and insist that you leave and live far away from us.

If you want to have a good marriage, then never marry for friendship.

If you marry at "your level or above," then you will have financial security.

If you tell your husband all of your secrets, then you will not have any leverage over him. (Remind me not to pass that last one down to my kids.)

Speaking of kids. . .

If you want to be happy in life, then make sure you have enough money to raise kids.

If you want to be happy in life, then make sure you have kids right away and the money will come. (Confusing, I know.)

If you want someone to take care of you in your old age, then you better have kids ASAP or else.

If you aren't having kids, then our lives will be incomplete.

Some of the rules were super dark and frightening.

If you don't get that mole checked out, then you might end up like our cousin's cousin who lost her arm to melanoma.

If you don't lock the door, then a murderer will come in at night just like he did in Unsolved Mysteries.

If you see your mom is not okay after Papou (grandpa) died but the relatives all tell you she is "fine" and to stop asking about it, then they must be correct and you must be wrong.

Some were just plain traumatic and haunt me to this day.

If I don't come back from the airplane, then you will be very loved by all of your relatives. (Insert fear of flying while needing to fly for a living. I told you it's complicated.)

If we yell at each other and are emotionally distant, then you are still going to be okay.

If you don't trust the "authority" in the room no matter what they say, then you're not going to be safe.

Some of them were very funny.

If you don't want to get sick, then keep the air-conditioning and fan off (or wear corduroys and turtlenecks).

If you want to be a polite girl, then always wear a headband.

If you don't want to have saggy back-fat like Yiayia (grandma), then never wear your bra too high or tight.

You get the gist, no? There were rules for everything. Some of the rules were repeated endlessly and explicitly while others were eerily silent yet always implied. As an award-winning "good girl," I knew where the line was and I never crossed it. Why?

Well, that's where the story of unraveling begins.

• • •

I *love* rules. I'm a master rule-follower. I am a Chief Executive Rule Abider. I love rules because they helped me make sense of my world as a little kid. I had no siblings, I was a "first" for many things in my Greek lineage, including being the first official American in our family. Rules made me feel like I was part of a family unit, a culture, a community. Rules ensured some type of safety, security, self-esteem—the biological trifecta that we all seek in our formative years.

Following the rules produced something so sweet it was worth its weight in gold. Following the rules came with the mecca of praise. The praise was subtle and benign at first:

"That was so nice."
"What a lovely little girl."
"She is such an old soul."

Hmmm… that felt good, look how happy my parents are, I don't often see them that happy. Let's try that again.

In adolescence, the praise came from multiple channels so often it felt like it was raining praise:

"She's my favorite student."
"So quiet and polite—she's a dream."
"I wish my kids were as good as you."

Cha-ching. My emotional validation bank account was soaring well into the six-figure territory at the ripe old age of fourteen.

Not only did I know how to work the system, I developed a winning formula:

Step 1 – Be quiet and/or polite and/or soft

Step 2 – Agree with all that is said by authority figure

Step 3 – Show up early to everything

Step 4 – Exemplify good manners

Step 5 – BONUS: Write a nice, hand-written 'thank you' note where appropriate

= **P R A I S E**

Into high school and college, praise became my go-to drug. I felt new and unusual sparks of wanting to dissent and debate a point of view but chose instead the meekness formula above. The result? Extra praise. I had the superpower of making every single person I interacted with feel like I was on their side. People seeing this behavior from the outside started to label this people-pleasing habit in language that impressed me: I was diplomatic, a great listener, emotionally aware, Switzerland, exceptional with people-dynamics, could instantly read a room, and was wise beyond my years. Another tasting menu of praise.

As college graduation sent me out into the real world, I was completely addicted to people-pleasing. I knew who and how to be when I interacted with every single stakeholder in my world. I knew what my parents needed to hear to keep them from fighting, I knew what my bosses needed to feel so that they would give me the projects I wanted, I knew what my friends needed to experience so that they would feel happy after a recent disappointment. I knew intuitively and exactly what the other party needed to experience in order to shift the dynamic back to neutral so I would once again feel safe, secure, liked, and praised.

> What started out as a simple set of enjoyable rules became the shackles that suffocated my authenticity.

An undesirable side effect of operating solely to make other people feel good around me was the dreaded, "You're so nice." Ugh. "Nice" became this identity that worked so well in the early years, only for me to be plagued by its shadow as I leapt into my twenties as an early working professional. "Nice" began to haunt me. All of a sudden, I was expected to have an opinion, to debate, to handle conflict. How? Why?! My harmonious-seeking insides suffered deeply and did the only thing they knew how to do— more people-pleasing. I kept agreeing. I kept flying under the radar so I wouldn't overshadow anyone or anything else while my insides went from simmering to brewing to bubbling. It was only a matter of time before I erupted.

I had meticulously and unintentionally built my very own "nice" prison. I knew how to be masterfully accommodating for everyone else in my world except for myself. What started out as a simple set of enjoyable rules became the shackles that suffocated my authenticity. A journal entry from that time encapsulates the intensity:

I have no idea who I am apart from how I make others feel when they're around me. I am merely a collection of other people's expectations and desires funneling through me. And I oblige because I know no other way.

Enter panic attacks (which I can now recognize as a strange portal into the early days of unraveling). After earning an all-consuming Executive MBA from Columbia University (while working full time) to please my father and beginning a very stressful work life as a digital strategy consultant at *The Economist* (more on that mismatch later, which sounded good and was on par with my people-pleasing, ambitious prison), I cracked.

The panic attacks arrived with the flip of a switch. I was "fine" and content in my insecure, overachieving world, until I wasn't. The attacks were awful, as anyone who has experienced the Universe urgently nudging them back on track knows. Some days I felt like an elephant was sitting on my chest. Other days, I became dizzy and disoriented out of nowhere. There was sadness, heaviness, dread. One unique flavor of these attacks was a newfound obsession with knowing where the nearest restroom was before leaving the house "just in case."

I canceled trips and gatherings with friends. I cut our honeymoon short because I was too scared to leave the hotel room in case the

And so began the pilgrimage back to myself.

overwhelm consumed me in a foreign country, lest we end up in a scary emergency room. More worry, more panic, more need for control. What on earth was happening?

They lasted about a year. Given what I've seen from clients and friends, I think I actually got off the overachieving, perfectionist, your-life-is-off-track train relatively unharmed. The thing I knew for sure was that there was no going back to "good girl." My health and wellness were at stake. And so began the pilgrimage back to myself. Therapy, coaching, acupuncture, Rolfing, Hellerwork, past-life regression, personality assessments, meditation, yoga, healers, journaling, shamanism, Reiki, craniosacral therapies, essential oils, nutritionists, mediums, Angels, tarot cards, personal retreats, sage. . . you name the healing modality, I tried it. For those laughing right now, of course I took an overachieving approach to squelching overachieving! I was relentless and obsessed. Finding myself again was the only thing that mattered, no matter the cost—and there *was* a cost.

The more I reclaimed pieces of myself with each passing month, the less other people liked it. I suppose that's part of how my "good girl" prison worked. I needed social validation to feel safe, yet I was trying to unlearn the need to please in order to find myself again. The time had arrived to face this enormous demon of needing to be liked. I was confronted with comments that ranged from the mild, such as, "You seem off," "You're not as happy as you normally are," and "Are you okay?" to the dramatic: "I don't even know who you are anymore," "I feel like you've abandoned us," "That's really selfish."

I had to laugh at the irony—my entire life up to this point had been oriented in a loss of self, and the moment I began to call in my own power, I was perceived as selfish. How fascinating to see the bright and shadow sides of how we show up in the world.

This unraveling chapter ends happily—and I am so grateful to have listened to the signs when I did. I took all of my pain and lessons learned and transmuted them into a space of discovery and healing. In all of my hunting to be the best, do the best, work for the best, learn from the best, I realized that "best" is an inside job. The outside in formula was a terrible trap: please everyone, do all the "right" things, work your ass off, and eventually you'll earn happiness. I'll save you some time—it's a dead-end. What I learned was that real happiness and success has nothing to do with earning or proving it. Leading one's life happens from the inside out. Leadership is an inner game—how you think, what you value, how you choose, what you stand for.

As I shared earlier, I bundled my lessons into my life's work and started a leadership development firm called *The Paradox of Leadership*. It's been just over a decade and I can proudly say that this business has been my biggest teacher and one of the great loves of my life. We have served thousands of people through executive coaching, training programs, and offsites and retreats. We work with organizations ranging from Fortune 500 companies and leading tech firms to international non-profits, women's advocacy groups, and pre-IPO start-ups. *What do I teach?* You guessed it—what I needed to learn most. I teach freedom. I teach people how to be more free in how they live, love, and lead.

I have always been a freedom-chaser. Perhaps freedom is the secret end-game for most die-hard rule-followers. What I didn't understand until recently was what I actually meant by "freedom." I always defined it as the inverse of something—the absence of fear, for example. (This is another side effect of years of forming my own opinions in response to what others had to say versus allowing them to stand on their own.) What triggered the fear? My relationship with time (never enough of it,

> Leadership is an inner game—how you think, what you value, how you choose, what you stand for.

never be late, never waste it), my relationship with money (never enough of it, never be late, never waste it), my relationship with professional success (never enough of it, never be late, never waste it). . . You get the point.

Through building and running my business, however, I solved for many of my previous confines of time, money, and success. I became the captain of my own fate: dictating my own schedule, enjoying untapped earning potential, and thriving with an impressive roster of exceptional clients. The day-to-day experience isn't so rosy, as any entrepreneur knows—but in broad terms, I was out of the corporate confines that felt stifling to me.

Even so, the freedom I experienced when starting my own company felt like a shell of actual freedom. Yes, I eliminated some obvious channels of people-pleasing and rule-following, but I was still at the mercy of my old inner narratives around fear-based worry and control. In fact, it was only in coming to terms with the whiplash and aftermath of the post-2020 world that I started to better understand what losing ambition and finding true freedom *actually* means. I suppose this is why so many spiritual teachers allude to the healing process as a spiral versus a straight line. We revisit the wounds over and over again—but with fresh eyes and a revived heart.

> Attunement, I've come to learn, is a process of coming back to oneself— one's own rhythms, frequencies, currents.

One of my longtime teachers uses the word "attunement" for the somatic healing work we do. I've always been intrigued by that word. What am I attuning to? Is there a "right" frequency, a "right" answer? Of course not. Attunement, I've come to learn, is a process of coming back to oneself—one's own rhythms, frequencies, currents. A hidden self that has always been there but buried and calcified by the ambitions of life—expectations, obligations, anxieties, routines, fears. A self that is tired of effort and might find ease and simplicity in the rules, but a self who also knows that attunement can help us traverse well beyond the surface shell of happiness. When I attune myself to who I really am and who I was put on this planet to be, I see the paradox in all its glory. Of course, it's all an inner game, and of course we get to rewrite the rules. At the end of the day, everyone is playing their own game of self-actualization. The question is—do we spend more time looking over our shoulders at others playing their game, or are we willing to do the work to invest in mastering our own?

What are the rules that you've lived by? Sometimes even the work of making the implicit explicit is enough to trigger the healing process. You can see how these stated and unstated rules of our lives have profound physical and emotional impacts. The rules run deep—some feel so commonplace to us that we can't imagine living or doing things another way. Start there. Question the ones that feel obvious and true. Ask yourself how they might look from a completely different vantage point or altitude. Consider what you are gaining and what you are losing by following these rules.

If you're like most of the leaders I work with, you're already starting to see the cost of the rules. You're feeling the burnout, noticing a disenchantment with your job and relationships, waiting for the next new thing to give you a surge of energy and satisfaction, planning your sabbatical from work and life. You're also profoundly wise and know that the next new thing is never going to be enough. The work of unraveling begins with the measuring stick. The rules you need to consider are like the little metric units on the stick—assessing, guiding, indicating how close or how far we are from a nondescript future state. Activate your courage and take an honest look at identifying the effects of the rules by which you live. It all starts here.

2
ASSESS THE BRIGHT AND SHADOW SIDE

I BELIEVE FIRST-GENERATION humans from any culture or context have a particularly complex relationship with ambition. Ambition is not only expected or demanded, it is a way of life. There is an inherent promise in being a "first" that one will do better than those who came before so that the familial, cultural, and generational strife and sacrifice will have been worth it. The scaffolding of ambition is sturdy and silent. "Firsts" tend to start running towards a life of goal achievement without taking a beat to assess in which direction ambition is pointing. They (meaning, *we*) board the ambition train without realizing they might hold a one-way ticket to nowhere.

> Ambition is not only expected or demanded, it is a way of life.

Like most immigrant communities, Greeks stick together like an amoeba when we find other Greeks. We could be on vacation in China and if we bump into another Greek there, we are assumed to be family. "Wait—you live in the United States? Do you know Jimmy Dimitrakopoulos—I think he lives in Chicago?!" The funny thing is when the other family actually *does* know Jimmy. It happens more often than you would think would be statistically possible.

My parents were fortunate enough to discover a handful of other good Greek families in our neighborhood in my very early childhood. There was no trial period, no dating period, no coffee chats—all of them were all in on Day One. With our actual families across the Atlantic in Greece, these Greek neighbors became (and are to this day) our *de facto* family. There was nothing unusual about graduating from strangers to cousins in an instant. We did everything together—from nursery and elementary school to activities, sleepovers, and camps, to weddings and funerals. This tight-knit Greek amoeba bolstered the illusion of safety and security very nicely.

One of the sightseeing highlights on the ambition train that is worth making a full stop to explore is the first-generation experience with education. Education, after all, is an insurance policy for many immigrant families. The parents make the sacrifice of moving to the United States (or elsewhere) so the children can be educated and be put on the path to a better life. You remember the rules.

Picking a middle school was a serious affair. Kindergarten and elementary schools were easy choices, based on the convenience of their locations since the stakes were low. Middle school was close to high school, which was a precursor to college, so the pressure was on. All of the Greek families gathered at one family's house for "the talk." There was food and drink and general merriment. Parents downstairs, ready to discuss our fate, and us kids upstairs, oblivious and content. The question of the evening: "Where should we send them to middle school?"

The public schools in our northern New Jersey county were considered less than average and didn't even make it into the conversation. To give us a leg up, private school was obligatory.

(After all, if it's expensive, it must be better, the Greek collective asserted.) There was discussion, debate, and lots of guesswork. They talked about the commutes, the money, the trajectory. One of the parents had heard from a lady at church that a prestigious high school in New York had very strong acceptance rates into top universities. And so it was decided over spanakopita that the whole slew of us would go to Horace Mann Prep School starting middle school.

As fate would have it, the admissions director was the one sole Greek in the administration of the school—young, handsome, and personable, no less. The parents basically set us up for a collective interview and quasi-threatened, quasi-instructed, "if you take one of them, you have to take all of them." As a fellow Philhellene, he agreed. (I think admissions processes were a bit "looser" in the '90s.) It was a done deal. As far as the parental units were concerned, they were setting us up in the best way they knew how—they bought us a first-class ticket on the education compartment of the ambition train. (We recently found out that our beloved admissions director has turned monk and lives on a remote island in Greece. I guess he got off the ambition train too!)

Another education season I remember vividly was the junior year college process. My parents and I were utterly clueless. Even worse, we knew that, unlike high school, where the amoeba could stick together for safety and security, college was a different ballgame. There was no Mr. Support-The-Greek-Kids to call up and secure a seat. I had an obligatory conversation with a counselor once every couple of months to ensure I had one or two "reach" schools and one or two "safety" schools, and that was about it in terms of strategy. My parents weren't able to help me with school work at this point, and the college search was not going to be any different.

So, I did what any immigrant "first" might do—I picked schools that would make my parents proud, selecting schools whose names lent them credibility. I applied to Harvard, Yale, Columbia, Princeton, Georgetown, NYU—and a bunch of "safety" schools a little bit further south and west of our Northeast corridor. I didn't know what I was doing, but I followed the steps. I wrote some good essays, took the SATs, and tried to do as many extracurricular activities as I could to make a compelling application. The envelopes streamed in—some small (rejections), some large (acceptances).

Here's how the decision point went down: My parents had some relatives in Maryland and we had visited Georgetown on a recent trip. We liked it—it was a beautiful campus and we ate at a nice restaurant nearby. Their friends had heard of Georgetown, so it had clout. It was near a relative if something dreadful happened to me, and it was a close enough drive from northern New Jersey if they needed to come and see me—all compelling components in our decision-making matrix. My dad's name is George and my mom's name is Georgette so we took that as the final sign. The Georgetown envelope was big, which meant I was in. We—yes, *we*—were going to Georgetown!

Fast-forward to a few years later, I graduated with an English major and Justice & Peace Studies minor. I know you're wondering, so, *yes*, I received Latin honors—*Magna Cum Laude*. (I don't mess around with this insecure, overachieving, blind ambition.) As expected, the "English major" thing was way too airy for the ambition train. After all, what do you do with that? Becoming a teacher, my dream since early childhood, was a prohibited career path as a "first" for obvious financial reasons. *More on that later.* So, I took the next page out of the ambition handbook and swung the pendulum the other way—an Executive MBA! My parents insisted that an MBA would provide me with the "hard skills" necessary to live a successful life. They didn't know what an MBA entailed and how misaligned it was with my skill set, but it sure sounded impressive. After two painful years of working full time, attending school all weekend, and feeling like a complete imposter, I got another piece of paper that mattered as a "first."

After Columbia—many breakdowns, panic attacks, and all-nighters later—the ambition train took me to the next logical stop: consulting. Consulting was something the Greeks could get behind. No one knew what consulting *actually* meant, but it sounded impressive nonetheless.

> There is a tricky and toxic quality about ambition.

So, I landed a job as a digital strategy consultant at *The Economist.* Wow, kudos Valia! Caveat—I didn't know the first thing about digital strategy. I am a pen and paper lady to this day. Also, I never read the magazine beyond looking at the cover. Thus commenced another season of life where my insides mismatched my outsides.

There is a tricky and toxic quality about ambition. It constantly requires more. More, for the sake of more. More, for the sake of "I should." There is always a higher mountain, a better degree, a more renowned school, a more impressive certificate, a more momentous achievement. When you are addicted to ambition for its own sake, however, these moments of accomplishment are often void of joy. Maybe you take a photo, post it on Instagram, frame the diploma and hang it in your room. Then what? Ambition becomes a game in and of itself. While we think it's about climbing one mountain peak, then the next, and then the next, until we've scaled the entire range, it's much sadder than this. It's not a beautiful mountain range in nature at all. This ambition is more like a treadmill set to a steep incline, going round and round, exhaustingly to nowhere.

I believe many firsts suffer from "ambition PTSD." This milestone mountain-climbing works well early in your career because there are plenty of opportunities in quick succession. You can jump from school to school to credential to advanced degree without stopping to sense the dis-ease building within. In mid-career, however, there are fewer mountains and seldom do they appear. There is only so much schooling and academic or credential success you can collect. After a point, you have to play the actual game of life—and stop preparing for it. This realization is loaded with feelings of fear, sadness, even loneliness. If I'm not here in service to you, that means I need to start the hard work of finding me.

When I'm working with self-proclaimed insecure, overachieving clients who are co-travelers on the train, I ask them to unravel their ambition so they can start claiming lost and numb pieces of themselves. I ask them: *Ambition, okay—but in service of what?*" This question calls ambition's bluff if there's no substance behind it.

For most, it's the "firsts" narrative on repeat. Ambition serves the sense of worthiness, the confidence façade, the family pride. A few levels down, there might be reasons revolving around money and providing for family or building a better life. For others, it's about ego. The job title and position at the company feel good. The club membership and street address validate their years and decades of effort. For a minority, it's about passion and experience—wanting to explore and appreciate their life to the fullest.

The question of ambition—*in service to what*—is a jarring one. It requires that your insides and your outsides have a real conversation. Jot it down in your notebook and sit with it for a minute. Maybe you too have found the paradoxical emptiness that comes with hyper achievement.

I've read more times than bears coincidence that the first half of our lives we live to *forget* who we really are, and the second half is lived to *remember* and reclaim who we really are. When I look back, I see what an integral part of the first half of my life on the ambition train played. It *was* my life. All of those schools and accolades and degrees served a purpose. When I started *The Paradox of Leadership* and was looking for speaking engagements to jumpstart my company, I found them with the familiar ease that comes with my valiant (Valia-nt!) effort. I was accepted to be a guest lecturer at Georgetown and Columbia about the power of personal (re)branding; I taught Executive MBA students at NYU Stern Business School the power of personal leadership and the inner work; I got invited to speak at several panels hosted by prestigious companies supporting women in business and women in leadership. The free speaking engagements led to coaching clients, which led to leadership team clients, which led to scaling my business beyond just me. I know that these doors opened with ease partly because my pieces of paper had some "good" names on them (thank you, ambition).

> What was once a strategy of insecurity became one of my biggest fortes as a coach.

I also know, in hindsight, how instrumental my people-pleasing niceness was in getting my business off the ground. While I thought "nice" was a painstakingly dull compliment, I now see the strategic likeability that it afforded me. People trust me instantly. Please feel safe and nurtured in my presence. While still at coaching school, I was able to secure several senior executives as clients partly because of this likeability. While other prospective coaches were working to impress during chemistry meetings, I was calm and connected. I knew what I was listening for to really allow the other person to feel seen and heard. What was once a strategy of insecurity became one of my biggest fortes as a coach. So, as

I look back and reflect on how I want to enter the "second" part of life—the reclaiming—, I see so many of the gems that were patiently waiting for their right time to emerge in their full and intentional power. I see how I needed blind ambition to master, ironically, what I now need to unlearn in order to find myself.

· · ·

So, fellow traveler, I'm curious about *you*. Where have you seen the bright sides of ambition really serve you and your path? There is no doubt that what is now about to unravel has supported you in some very meaningful ways throughout the years and decades. This acknowledgment of the good behind our kryptonite is essential. It is often the fuel that allows us to propel ourselves to the peaks of the mountains we choose to scale. It appreciates the effort and offers gratitude for the endless pursuit of working to find who we are and what we want to do on this earth. Find the good and bow to it in a moment of reverence. It will soften its grip when you can look it straight in the eyes and say, "thank you."

3
REKINDLE YOUR STRENGTHS

I KNEW AT the age of six I was going to be a teacher despite the first-generation headwinds to the contrary. (There was a quick pediatrician detour, but fainting at the sight of blood ruled that out pretty quickly.) I would line my dolls up and want to teach them all sorts of things. I would share what I learned at school, read from my books, ask them questions. I am told my lessons were mostly incoherent, but nonetheless entertaining. One day, around the holidays, my mom recalls me yelling at one of my dolls, "Sit down, Hanukkah! Be quiet, Hanukkah!" It was a sheltered Greek immigrant life and I missed the cue that Hanukkah was a holiday and not the name of a classmate-turned-doll.

Throughout elementary school, the thing I wanted most in the world was a chalkboard. One Christmas, my wish was granted. I would practice writing with my right and left hand for hours. Writing in block font, erasing, writing in script, erasing—pure bliss. In fourth grade, I remember wanting to practice the most complicated word I could think of to show my ambidextrous talents. Thanks to *Teenage Ninja Mutant Turtles*, I landed on *Cowabunga Shredhead*. I would pour myself a mug of Coca-Cola to pretend I was drinking coffee just like my favorite teacher, Mrs. Toby. I would tape little strips of paper to my nails so I could mimic her Lee press-on nails (it was the '80s, in case you didn't pick that up). I would attempt to click the silent paper nails on my little table to get my friends' attention during a playdate. Off I went, writing *Cowabunga Shredhead* endlessly on the chalkboard. Right hand, erase, left hand, erase. Could life be any sweeter?

Sometimes, I would wear dresses like the teachers; other times I would decorate my room the way our classroom was decorated at school. The love of the chalkboard expanded to an obsession with all things writing—fancy pens and pretty paper, erasers from the *Hello Kitty* store, notebooks with lines, pencils and sharpeners. If it had to do with teaching, I had to have it. A few years later, I graduated from a chalkboard to a whiteboard fully equipped with an easel, stand, markers, and a carrying case. I was in the big leagues. It was worth all the practice, by the way. To this day, I am known amongst clients and colleagues alike for my Grade A facilitation flip charts. (This is the type of compliment that never makes it on a resume, but fills me with deep joy and pride.)

As I mentioned, though, becoming a teacher was a no-go for a first-generation Greek kid. After all, my parents did not sacrifice everything to fuel my education ambition train for me to go and educate others and make no money while doing it (or so I was told). I remember taking personality assessments at the career center at Georgetown to figure out what on earth I wanted to do once I graduated, since teaching was off the list. All signs pointed to a "helping people" profession—HR, corporate trainer, social worker, psychologist. I remember calling my sole American family member, my aunt Dianne, to ask about HR since my parents had no idea what it was. She consulted at a top bank so her opinion carried a lot of weight in our home. Instructed by the family, she confirmed that HR was not for me. Case closed. None of the professions that aligned with who I was passed the first-generation test.

When something is embedded in your soul, however, the gravitational pull never goes away. My aspirations merely remained dormant until I was brave enough to turn on the light and dust off the cobwebs. There's a reason something is called a "calling." It calls us—or rather, beckons us. Silently, at first, and then like a constant humming. I found myself (effortlessly) becoming the unofficial in-house "teacher" for every company I worked for—running ad hoc workshops, counseling my bosses to unlock their potential, bringing teams together to discuss their interpersonal dynamics. While this wasn't my day job, it was certainly where I found most of my energy and work that played to my natural talents.

If we don't listen to our calling, it gets louder and louder to ensure we don't miss our exit for aligning our passions with our purpose. This story, despite its twists and turns, ends mostly happily. I manifested the ending and became a teacher after all. Rather than teaching elementary school students, I teach corporate executives. Rather than writing on a classroom chalkboard, I write on portable flip charts at offices and retreat centers throughout the country. I became who I always was.

> When something is embedded in your soul, however, the gravitational pull never goes away.

Aspiring coaches often reach out to learn about how I got to where I am. I'm always happy to take time and answer questions, but I don't really enjoy talking about it. Perhaps I haven't fully healed from all of the people-pleasing, inauthentic choices along the way. The story feels clunky to me, jagged, even, but the story is mine and it brought me to a place of professional align-ment—which is more than most people can say. In fact, I have an embarrassing statistic in my work as an executive coach and leadership development professional. I don't really speak about this data point (and it's probably one I'm most proud of): I have a very high percentage of clients who leave their jobs within a few weeks or months of working with me or seeing me speak.

The pickle here is that I get paid by their organization to make them better at their job *within* the organization. It's not that I coax them out, yell doomsday, or pressure a change in any way. In fact, I'm not attached at all to a particular outcome. What I have learned to do really well as a coach, however, is what I learned to do for myself through the first few stages of losing my ambition. I see people. I see them for what's real in their lives, who they could be, what the world is waiting for that only they can mani-fest. A homecoming, if you will. A surrender to their calling.

One of the common questions I get during a session when the client is embarking on their inner work is: "What if I don't know what my passion is?" You might be thinking and feeling the same thing. Sigh. Few of us know off the bat because there is so much noise in our heads from the ambition addiction that, in the *I want to* versus *I have to* debate, the latter always wins. Responsibility trumps desire. Busy-ness eats rest for dinner. Accolades defeat the simple joys of enough. Despite this, the inner teacher (or pilot or astronaut or chef or artist or entrepreneur) doesn't dis-appear. He or she just learns to lurk in the shadows until there's an opportunity to make an appearance. While the answer isn't always clear, there are plenty of clues along the way. Even in hindsight, noticing the clues will reinforce them to keep showing up brighter and louder.

If you're barreling along on the ambition train to nowhere, or you're wondering why you're stuck in pangs of loneliness or emptiness, hand the keys over to your internal energy barometer. I've learned that trusting it unlocks an entirely different relationship with self-worth. So, if you're always drained after a certain type of task, and this task makes up 80% of your workday, you're probably in a bit of a professional mess. If, on the other hand, you notice that every time you help a colleague with a certain type of problem, you are buzzing with ideas the rest of the day, then pick up that clue and follow it. Our energy is like a compass that always redirects us back to our true north. While our brain can create sabotaging mental chatter to veer us in the wrong direction, our energy is a neutral force that can't be easily hijacked. I always think about this as one of those metal detector rods that you see some random people holding on a beach. They are searching for the gems—keep listening for the beeps.

Even if I wanted to kick teaching to the curb—and I tried many times—it found me. When I lost track of time or was deep in flow, I was always engaging in some type of teaching activity—whether for myself or others. It came easily to me. Our strengths are a funny thing. We're taught to focus on weaknesses and gaps from early childhood. Greeks are no exception to this rule—in fact, I think we might be leading the work-on-your-weaknesses parade.

> Our energy is like a compass that always redirects us back to our true north.

I was never good at math. My operations-minded father would hover over me ready to give out praise for a right answer and agitated disapproval for a wrong answer when I would do my math homework. He had me sit at his desk and do practice math problems on a yellow pad with a mechanical pencil, over and over and over again. The disapproval turned to frustration and then anger pretty quickly. I think it was a kind of sport for him—but torture for me. The floppy disc games I got for Christmas to enjoy on our family's first computer were all math quizzes. What fun! Geometry and calculus in high school remained a foreign language no matter which way I tried to shift my learning approach. My math skills remained mediocre at best. You should have seen what a delight I was taking managerial statistics and accounting during my MBA at Columbia. *Send help!*

On the other hand, I was really good at writing while I was growing up. I enjoyed writing of all sorts—essays, research assignments, creative projects. Words intrigued me, and communicating through language felt like a royal treat. I ended up writing my thesis at Georgetown on the English language itself. My school books had rainbows of annotations along the margins. Ideas, stars, and exclamation points highlighted the important messages, reminders of possible connections to other chapters. The messier, the better. So, given my weakness in math and my strengths in writing, do you think I got a math tutor or a writing tutor? One guess.

We're wired as a society to improve weaknesses rather than develop strengths. While it was historically a grasp at survival and made logical sense, it is now an expiring mode of leveraging one's abilities throughout life, I believe. The sad truth is, there is no number of tutors or amount of money or time you could have thrown at my math gap to make me an expert. At best, I became competent. However, imagine if the same worry, time, resources, and attention went towards my innate strength. What would have been possible in those formative career years? I would certainly have started my authorship before the age of forty.

Cultivating strengths and investing in those strengths is a language of personal leadership. Thankfully, more and more companies are ascribing to this truth that matching people in jobs that highlight their strengths is a way to keep employees happier *and* make the organization more successful and productive. There are plenty of books and experts in this space of strength-based leadership, so I'll leave it at this: the minute you have the courage to slow down enough to notice and honor your gravitational pull (whether your strengths, your brighter energy, or your memories of who you were before the world told you otherwise), that is where the journey of self-actualization can really begin. *Cowabunga shredhead*, indeed.

4

GET CURIOUS

IN ONE OF the women's leadership programs I facilitate, we ask the participants to introduce themselves by talking about a woman they admire or who has shaped their life in a meaningful way. It's a beautiful entry point through which they can dive deep and quickly build authentic connections before the days of hard work ahead. Most women talk about their mothers, grandmothers, a mentor, and occasionally a public figure. They share stories of resilience and pain, hope and fortitude.

I have an incredibly close relationship with my mother. She has been "my person" throughout my life. For some reason, however, in the dozens of programs I've run for this client, I never mention her as my "inspiring woman." I might pick a client, my first coach, a neighbor. At first, I thought it was me trying to be "different" so that I could model variety to the participants, but that was a cheap excuse. I really began to wonder why I never happily shared a story or anecdote about this most meaningful person in my life—the woman who literally shaped the human being I am. In my inquiry, I discovered something perturbing. It turns out that I never called out my mother because I was harboring a secret resentment. In a program centered around finding one's voice and unleashing strength, I resented that my mother did not walk her own talk.

My mother is the type of mother that has blinders on when it comes to me. Perhaps because I am her only child, but I think it's more than that. The glasses through which she sees the light I bring into the world aren't just rose-colored, they're straight up hot pink. From early childhood, to the awkward teenage years, to escaping to Australia for a semester abroad, to starting a business, to moving across the country—there is not a single thing that she believes is impossible for me to achieve, create, or experience. She's the mother who would leave me notes in my lunchbox about becoming President one day, an astronaut on another. The bizarre resentment ate at me for months, making me wonder what could be causing it. Program after program, I mentioned other women and their impact in my life, all the while pushing my mother into the corners of my mind and heart.

It recently dawned on me—and it was a complicated thread of unraveling ambition. I was angry because, while she saw an abundant, limitless, extraordinary life for me, she didn't choose that for herself. I was angry that she gave up on her aspiring floral design business—*The Gracious Table*—because she didn't want to miss getting me ready for school in the mornings. I was irritated that she stopped her attempts at running a marketing business she had started in Greece because she didn't want to travel too much and be away from me. She got a college degree at sixty, had a passion (and talent) for painting, wanted to write and tell her story—and didn't. She never put herself and her needs out in front. I was annoyed that everything she wanted to do, she avoided or postponed for fear of strife with my father (or perhaps with herself). She would tell me, "Go! Dream! Explore! Create!

Unlock!" and yet model a life that felt small, afraid, disappointed, and empty.

My words are harsh, but this was the anger and resentment speaking on loop: *How could she let me down by not walking her own talk, by not upholding the standards she had for me, for herself?*

Then I became a mother.

After my daughter was born, I whizzed back to work. After all, that's what a responsible, ambitious, overachieving human who runs a business does, right? Besides, there is no such thing as an entrepreneur's paid maternity leave, and my husband was furloughed along with the rest of the travel industry during the pandemic. If I didn't work, I imagined the ceiling would cave in on my safety and security—and on that of my now-growing family.

Barely able to sit up from the C-section, I checked emails, got back to clients, and put myself at the bottom of my exhausting list of to-dos. This isn't a statement to forge sympathy or admiration. It was a choice I made—and it was a regrettable one. About six months into Emilia's life, when summer and overwhelm arrived, I broke. There was not an ounce of anything left to give to any-one, except to the six-month old creature for whom I was *actually* responsible. So, I took a delayed maternity leave with a summer off (well, summer turned to just the month of August—old ambi-tion habits die hard). In these delicious few weeks, I said goodbye to the computer with a clever out-of-office notice that made people smile and made my only priority baby music class, baby playgroup, baby swim class—and anything else that started with "baby." She was my summer project. Becoming a mother (not just having a baby) was my truth.

The month was unforgettable. The days were long and delightful. She learned to crawl, started eating solid food, and threw her hand up in the air and grunted every time she saw another human, which made for a very funny and awkward sign of greeting. We laughed, we napped, we played, we pooped. It was glorious. All I wanted was more of it. All I wanted was for the world to disappear, for work to go away, for looming thoughts of financial responsibility to disappear like a bad dream, for my rumbling ambition to just turn off.

Throughout this little baby sabbatical, I heard myself saying:

"Nothing else matters when I'm with her."
"I just want to be with her."
"My most important job on earth is being present with her."

Then it hit me like a tsunami. My mom may not have wanted to be the President or an astronaut, but when I look back on my childhood (and adulthood), my mother was always there for me. I mean, *always*. There was not a single play or recital or sporting event or graduation or breakup or ceremony or dinner or airport pickup that my mother was not present and accounted for.

She was "a woman who inspired me" because my world did not exist without her as its backdrop and canvas. She chose presence and attention as her superpowers. They may not have included the bells and whistles that I would have wanted for her, but I don't think I would have had the audacity to even *make* such a claim were my esteem not built by her being there in a foundational way for every moment of my life. And that is a gift beyond measure.

So, at the client program immediately following my "Summer of Baby," I shared that the woman who inspired me the most was my mother. I cried and didn't apologize. The other women cried. The program was probably one of the best we've had. She inspired me not because of what she did or didn't do, but by shaping my life through the sheer power of presence and the magic of always being there. To give someone the feeling of being held, witnessed, seen—I think there is no greater gift. This is something that I want my daughter to experience through me. And I will tell her that this was a gift bestowed by her grandmother.

> Our brains can't hold the energies of judgment and curiosity at the same time.

• • •

I invite you to think about what might start mattering more than ambition in *your* life. Or perhaps where ambition might take a back seat to something more vulnerable, less obvious, more gentle—presence, wellbeing, community, peace, for starters. Sometimes these full circle moments allow us to see the evolution of our thinking—from the early stages of assumptions and habits to the later reflections of self-awareness and humility, growth and learning.

One of my all-time favorite coaching nuggets is that our brains can't hold the energies of judgment and curiosity at the same time. They neutralize each other. So, if you find yourself feeling judgmental towards a person, a season, or a circumstance, try inviting curiosity in. What patterns are repeating? What are you not seeing here? Where is there room to see this differently? This tool of shifting from judgment to curiosity is what allowed me to better understand my mother's superpower of presence rather than judging her as not enough in her life. My own ambitious judgments, assumptions, and interpretations skewed my lens of empathy for and understanding of others. Unraveling ambition—or any blinding force in our lives—requires us to get really curious and be willing to see the same situation from a completely different vantage point. And what beautiful gifts get seeded in the process.

5
GET COURAGEOUS

COURAGE SEEMS TO poke its head out towards the middle of the unraveling journey, after you've done some very effective excavating and are gearing up to set the foundation for what lies ahead. What's tricky about courage is that we all experience it (or a lack of it) in unique ways. As such, it tends to be one of the lonelier aspects of unraveling—you start wondering if it's just you. What might require profound courage for one person is a non-issue for someone else. Think about when you've been called to the arena to slay your dragons. Was it battling your negative mental chatter? Facing a health scare? Ending a relationship? Dealing with unimaginable loss? Starting a business despite unfavorable headwinds? My call to courage came in an unlikely package.

. . .

On January 8, 2020, a large FedEx box landed at my door. In it was the key to everything I had always wanted but kept quiet in my heart—motherhood. Using this key to unlock motherhood also meant facing my deepest fear. This box had varied contents (and should have come with a warning sticker rather than a "fragile / keep refrigerated" sticker). There were about 250 syringes

packed in bags of twenty– all different sizes and thicknesses ranging from ½ inch and thin to 4.5 inches and thick. There were more
medications than the "Cold & Flu" section at Walgreens—some to
be refrigerated, some kept at room temperature, some to be
given at an exact minute, and others in a general a.m. and p.m.
fashion. Alcohol swabs and a few plastic bins to dispose of the
needles served as accessories in the box. As my brain processed
the sheer volume of what I would
need to put into my body to have a
baby, I began viscerally shaking. I'm
the person whose most aggressive
interaction with pharmaceuticals is a
single Tylenol if I'm keeled over in pain—about two or three times
in my four-ish decades of life.

Unraveling requires us to face our shadows and fears.

My resistance to the chemistry experiment that would ensue in
my ovaries was the "easy" part to overcome. More terrifying was my
sheer dread of needles and anything doctor-related. I'm not alluding
to a mild discomfort and preference. I'm talking about an extreme
phobia laced with a history of navigating medical encounters with
avoidance, denial, anxiety, shaking, hyperventilating, fainting, vom-
iting—rinse and repeat—for as long as I can remember.

I'll pause to offer the punchline up front as we dive in: unraveling requires us to face our shadows and fears. We are asked
to consider what lies on the other side of our fears and what we
might need to overcome in order to live and lead the life we want
most. This work is not easy and is certainly not for the faint of
heart (no pun intended). Your mountain might look very similar
to mine, or completely different. What I'd urge you to look for
are where your fears have gripped you into a way of being that
no longer serves you. Consider for yourself what type of courage,

or perseverance, or surrender it might take to unlock some of the darkest parts of your belief structures. Deep breath. Let's go.

My childhood nemesis was Dr. E. She was a strong Egyptian woman who would try to knock the fear out of me with unfunny jokes and smacking tongue depressors on my knees to lighten my mood every time we had a visit. The stories of my Dr. E dread are endless: I would cruise through the eye exam at the annual physical only to physically tackle her in an attempt of dodging the looming vaccinations; blood draws inevitably led to fainting and smelling salts to revive me; once, I had a bad poison ivy encounter and decided to hide it from my mom by wearing turtlenecks and long pants to school for two days so I wouldn't have to go to the doctor. Inevitably, it spread to my neck and face and I lived the next week in oatmeal baths and oral steroids; I remember taking out the trash as my fourth grade classroom chore when a piece of glass protruding from the black bag gashed my knee pretty badly. Rather than telling the teacher or nurse, I spent the afternoon in the bathroom wiping off the blood and doing some paper towel patchwork so my mom wouldn't see the wound and take me to the pediatrician. I wonder how her staff flagged my chart.

IVF was a choice I had put off for seven years. At thirty-three, I felt like there was plenty of time to change our eating habits, nip my husband's drinking habits, visit every alternative healing modality possible, and pray so that I could will a baby into this world without having to go through "my last resort." The irony is, I *knew* IVF would work (I'm cognizant that not every person or couple can say this or has this privilege). In my heart of hearts, I knew the ICSI process was our guarantee to have a baby—but that was no solace as I stared at this box. My dragon to slay *was* the process, and the time had arrived. Forty felt like the final stop—it was now or never and I decided that I wanted a baby more than I wanted to assuage my fear. Yet another opportunity for my ambitious insides to do this the hard and effort-full way. Sigh.

So we began, my husband relatively steady, and me white-knuckling it the whole way. We got into a pretty good rhythm after the first couple of weeks of terror and tears. We had our protocol sheet with specific details on timing, medication, and injections, and we followed it to a tee. I am a good, overachieving student, after all. As those who have undergone IVF or some version of it know all too well, the capstone experience is the dreaded progesterone-in-oil injections that essentially serve as nourishment for the embryo in the first few months of development. We perfected our process over the course of the quarter:

Step 1 – Collective sigh right after breakfast and dinner. Catch each other's gaze. Nod. Silently affirm, *it's time.*

Step 2 – Grab the frozen kale from the freezer to numb my behind—top outer quadrant. Simultaneously heat the neck pillow filled with farro in the microwave for a minute to help soothe the site after the injection. (The smell of burnt grains from the neck pillow nauseates me to this day).

Step 3 – Gracefully bend over the edge of bed (more like plop with agony). Brené Brown has nothing on vulnerability until you've been in this position waiting for an intramuscular shot of thick and oily progesterone.

Step 4 – Micromanage my husband with directions: "Make sure you get it in the circle," "You missed yesterday and it hurt," "That spot is bruised, move over an inch," "Try at a

ninety degree angle because sideways might hit the nerve."
(The nurse at the fertility clinic drew some circles with a black
Sharpie on the upper right and left quadrants of my butt for
target practice and extra directional assistance. We needed it.)

Step 5 – Scrunch my eyes and count down from 10 to 1. (The
oil takes forever to dispense and no, deep breathing and
soothing music does not work for this process.)

Step 6 – Grab our Boston Terrier Henry's tennis ball and
rub the spot vigorously for five minutes to avoid leaving a
clumpy, bumpy, painful oil residue bump on the inside. Apply
heat from the neck pillow and rest. Collective sigh; we're
done for the next 12 hours.

We made progress, we got better, and my butt looked like a
black-and-blue mountain range by the end of the six months. We
got through it.

There were funny moments throughout this IVF experience,
of course: the dog getting involved and taking my graceful position as an invitation to play; me trying to administer one needle
into my right thigh for two and a half hours just to "prove" that
I could do it—my cortisol spiked so high I zonked out for twelve
hours straight (there were many tears mixed with cheerleading
mantras, but I never got the needle to touch my skin); being on a
work trip and needing to hire a local med student to come to my
hotel room at night to administer the injection—I'm sure the front
desk thought I was quite the promiscuous leadership trainer.

One of the funniest memories I have of our IVF process was a
virtual talent show we had with a group of new California friends

to pass the time. (You'll recall Spring 2020 was the season the world shut down, so virtual gatherings were all the rage until our eyeballs got serious screen fatigue and wanted nothing to do with Zoom.) Some families dressed up in Halloween costumes, others did a karaoke song or two. We were so entrenched in IVF-mode that when it was our turn, we shared that our best current talent was our injection process—finessed for weeks—and we would be happy to illustrate if the children got off the screen. We laughed, we cried, we ached for this baby, we prayed, we got boatloads of solicited and unsolicited advice, and we oriented our entire life around the bi-weekly, weekly, or daily doctor's visits and pricks and prods.

Fast-forward to gameday. March 13th, 2020—our embryo transfer day. To think of the precision, science, medicine, and orchestration of every single cell of my body that was required for a successful outcome blows my mind. But what inspires my heart is the sacred space where science met spirituality. The embryology lab closed due to COVID that following Monday, March 16th. If every moment and procedure and injection and prayer and tear hadn't lined up exactly to the tee, we would have never transferred our baby Emilia that day. She may have never come to be. Tears drench my laptop as I'm typing this—even after the countless times I have shared chapters of our fertility story. I didn't understand the "wonder" in the word "wonder-ful" until I lay there waiting and witnessing a microscopic five-day embryo (the toil of months, years of infertility struggle) being transferred into a scientifically perfected uterus and knowing, from that moment on, it was in the hands of God. Science and spirituality, ambition and trust, effort and

> The sacred space where science met spirituality.

surrender—in that moment and every sonogram and heartbeat thereafter.

Enamored by the magic we saw under the microscope that day, we started speaking to the embryo each night before bed. We would read a children's book, send her our prayers, and say: "Goodnight Embryo #1." Those who have experienced IVF know that once the viable embryos are returned from the lab, they stack rank them from the strongest to the weakest and are given complex codes to differentiate. She was #1 on the list. Night after night, "Goodnight Embryo #1—we love you."

About a month after we knew the process had been success-ful and had gotten through all the books we had received, we started talking names. "We can't keep calling her Embryo #1," I told my husband. He assured me that we could—and said "let's shorten it to Emmy." She had stuck—literally and figuratively—in our hearts. It was her name from the moment we saw her under the microscope. It was a name that would honor every step of the journey and what it took to bring her into the world. Careful not to obscure her Greek roots, we backed into a name that worked in both Greek and English. From Embryo #1 to Emmy to Emi to Emilia.

Now, let's be clear that losing ambition is a *process*, not a *moment*. As an ambitious mother-to-be, I/we prepared tirelessly for a beautiful hypnobirthing experience. Eight weeks of a virtual course with other local couples attempting a smooth, unmed-icated, magical birth. We learned about birthing positions and studied different chemicals released in the body during birth. We practiced breathing techniques and discussed our roles and the role of a doula throughout the journey. We studied the text and did the exercises.

Alas, our sweet Emilia thought it would be fun to give mommy a final test of breaking through her fear of doctors and needles by positioning herself in breech. We tried to make her budge in every way possible—an External Cephalic Version at the hospital to "go in" and turn her (please skip it—horrific experience), lying upside down on an ironing board (fun way to watch TV), heating up my pinky toe with Chinese medicine moxibustion incense (ouch) to have her turn on her own. Nada. This girl wanted to come into the world in a way I would remember forever. My grand finale of losing control and surrendering to trust was concluding this IVF chapter with my most dreaded outcome, a C-section. (Yes, we got a 50% refund from the unnecessary doula and unused hypnobirthing class.)

> True wonder lives on the other side of fear, with courage serving as the bridge between the two.

I fainted as they tapped my spine in preparation, of course, but after weeks of effort and angst to do it "my way," I let go. I knew this was one thing that was completely out of my hands. Time to trust and surrender. November 20th, 2020 at Hoag Hospital in Newport Beach, California—my heart took its first deep breath as Baby Emilia took hers. I finally experienced the real meaning of the word called "wonderful."

I believe that the word "wonderful" is one of the most overly misused words in the English language—and I'm a chief offender. We throw it around so lightly and carelessly sometimes—a wonderful cup of coffee, have a wonderful day, that was a wonderful book, what a wonderful idea. But do we really mean wonderful—seeped in and full of wonder? No way. Think about what "wonder" elicits in you. Awe. Time-stopping. Something divine or sublime. Other-worldly. Undeniable presence. I am pretty certain that true wonder lives on the other side of fear, with courage serving as the bridge between the two.

A recent update on my now head-to-toe-dressed-in-pink toddler is that she decided to change her name. After our entire journey through courage and into wonderful, she rewrote the script. Talk about a human being who already knows the importance of finding her voice in the world! She decided at one and a half years old that "Mia" suited her more than "Emi" as a nickname. So, as she's begun to speak, she is declaratively Mia. In Greek, it means "the one." She really is wonderful.

6

STAY ON YOUR OWN JOURNEY

I'VE MADE IT my business to be the boss of other people's journeys. While this has made for a fruitful career as an executive
coach and unofficial therapist to many in my life, like anything
steeped in ambition, it has also cost me. The lines between what
was and wasn't mine to solve started blurring at too young of
an age. Feeling responsible for my parents' marriage set me on
a decades-long journey of gripping, fixing, and desperately con-
structing harmony wherever I could, no matter how wobbly the
foundation. There was no separation between my journey as their
child and their journey as a seemingly unhappy couple.

No surprise from the universal psychology 101 textbook, I
replicated similar dynamics in my own relationships years later. I
found men who needed fixing and relationships that felt like constant work. If I made them feel complete by helping them, they
would stay forever and my harmony-seeking insides would rest
another season. Their journeys became my life's purpose—help
a little here, coach and inspire a little there, motivate and teach,
grow and evolve, urge and cheer. And while we're all up for a

little development as human beings, my attachment to development was an addiction—an ambition addiction. Perhaps ambition seems innocuous compared to substance abuse or means of self-soothing more universally recognized as destructive, but I believe it holds the same dark shadows—and thus requires the same kind of attention.

My husband's self-soothing drug of choice was alcohol. Like many hardworking Greek immigrants, his parents were in the Greek diner business. You've all seen the movie, so you know how Greek diners go—it's not a job, it's a way of life. It's a 365, 24/7 life—we always joke that their first child was the family diner on 84th Street and Madison Avenue in Manhattan. And it's not a joke—

> My attachment to development was an addiction—an ambition addiction.

forty years of tireless dedication and sacrifice to the only life they knew—servitude. Alcohol was often a family's way of coping with the realities of this harsh life. It was a reward, a moment to unwind after a long and stressful day. Unsurprisingly, my husband followed suit. The thought of inheriting this life he didn't want was a lot to handle, I imagine. This is something familiar that most first-generation kids have to face. It is the ultimate dragon to slay: disappointing our parents to find ourselves.

While I wouldn't describe my husband as an alcoholic, when he *did* drink, there was overindulgence. It was usually family affairs or special occasions. As someone who is quite prudish with alcohol, I was in a constant loop of feeling disappointment, anger, and resentment, which kicked my fix-it mode into full gear. We argued past each other for years on this topic, beginning with our wedding day when we left our party not on speaking terms. I controlled, he resisted, and the dance went on for years.

On March 1, 2019, after a fateful episode of prolonged hiccups due to a Pisco Sour indulgence at 10,000 feet on Machu Picchu, Peru (a story for another time), he decided to choose sobriety. Whether it was our history of pain around this topic, my constant nagging, fear of following his family's footsteps with alcohol, or his decision to prioritize his wellness after our move to California, I'll never know—probably a combination. At first, his sobriety felt like a personal victory for me. I won! After all of the pain, I was finally vindicated, and our perfect life could now begin. Ha!

What ensued was the most painful year of my life. The ambition queen had zero control of where, how, and when his recovery would ensue, and I imagine he felt the very same way, just from a different lens. This turbulent year was exacerbated by the fact that we both had deep shame around the topic, so we held it very close to the vest, causing a vicious cycle of loneliness and isolation. As he worked to find new sober communities, my resentment grew lonelier and louder. I bought into the illusion that he did this for me and that the decision would instantly bring us closer. Instead, it ripped us apart, a little more each day. I never understood the phrase "death by a thousand paper cuts" until that fateful year. I demanded closeness and he required freedom. I wanted to make up for all the lost time and he wanted to figure out who he was without a numbing agent. I expected joyful planning for our future and he had opened the Pandora's box of his consciousness and was unraveling all of its contents.

I'm not an expert on addiction, but what I perceived was that he needed to replace alcohol with something else. I was hoping that "something else" would be me, our hopes for starting a family at the time, travel. Instead, it became about resolving his deepest desire from childhood—being in a body that he could be proud of. He spent the year transforming his physique. From running and cycling, to lifting and pickleball, to making friends with trainers and joining training gyms, he created a new world. The problem was, I didn't make it into the transformation equation. The resentment and grief overflowed in my heart—I felt that I had tirelessly supported the 1.0 version of my husband only to be left behind and excluded from the 2.0 version.

Our arguments were comical (in hindsight, of course). We would talk past and through each other. I didn't understand his new world and he didn't realize the impact his new world was having on me. I silently seethed while he felt the need to walk on eggshells to protect himself from my quiet wrath. We talked it out, and tried again and again and again. All the while—the fertility clock was like a pressure valve ticking in the background.

In the end, my husband's sobriety decision propelled him into a year of losing over seventy-five pounds and sculpting his body to the point of impressive. He faced demons from the past and worked through not only finding himself, but also liking himself. His journey was remarkable, and watching him transform himself—without me—was both awe-inspiring and frightening.

Recall that the strategy around my fixing and helping held an implicit guarantee—if they need me and I help them, they will stay. My husband's solo journey through sobriety left me with a perpetual paranoia that this was the beginning of the end. Once he was "fixed," I would be left behind. It makes me sad to write that statement "out loud"—but it is true and this was a linchpin moment in losing my ambition to save everyone and their mother, even if that someone was my husband. As our couple's therapist once told me—a sting I still remember—"Valia, you need to love and trust yourself more than you're afraid to lose him."

· · ·

Trust is a concept I have really come to understand these past few years. Whether in my marriage or in my work with clients, there is nothing without trust. Trust allows us to ease into the present moment without schlepping the weight of the past or the anxiety of the future. Trust affords honesty, truth-telling, and naming what is (versus projecting what could be). The funny thing about trust is that we assume it's one-size-fits-all. We imagine that we experience trust in the same ways. This could not be further from the truth.

Trust is a language—like the recently popularized love languages. Some of us need credibility, authority, and history to build trust. Others need reliability and consistency over time. Still others need to know one's motivation is pure or that they can connect on a more emotional and connected level before proceeding. There are countless trust languages and indicators and we get ourselves into trouble when we assume that our way is the only way. The work we do at *The Paradox of Leadership* literally unravels the trust dynamics

> Trust allows us to ease into the present moment without schlepping the weight of the past or the anxiety of the future.

between leaders and their teams to help them better understand how to grow their impact from a very solid foundation. I wish I knew then what I know now about trust. Another reminder that we teach what we need to learn most.

A mantra that helped me slowly but surely loosen the grip of fear, reclaim my authentic confidence, and activate trust to recalibrate the space between my husband's heart and mine during this chaotic time was this: **stay on your own journey**. This mantra is something that is directed inwardly—a friendly reminder to

myself that I need to be responsible for my own feelings and contributions to any situation. *Valia, stay on your own journey.*

However, it is also directed outwardly. For example, if I feel
his stuff (or anyone's stuff for that matter) encroaching on my
personal boundaries, it's something useful to recalibrate any ten-
dencies towards unhealthy enmeshment. It sets an immediate
emotional boundary. *Hey you, stay on your own journey.* See? It
works both ways! I have repeated these words more than once
under my breath as a gentle separation of codependent energies
that can get mixed up and messy.

A pleasant side effect that I wasn't expecting from this lesson
of losing my ambitious grip was the quiet emotional freedom I
started discovering inside. By staying on my own journey, I found
a lot more time in the creases and cracks of my day that would
otherwise be spent sending a helpful text, checking in, offering a
book, writing a thoughtful email.
It's not that I don't do these things
anymore, but I do them by choice,
not by necessity. Some of that
space was dedicated to bringing
this book into the world. First we need to remember what our
own journey is about and then we take a few courageous steps
towards it each day.

> Detached involvement
> offers a new opportunity
> for engagement.

There was a term I learned in coaching school that feels relevant to share here: **detached involvement**. I teach this concept
a lot to our clients and many have held onto it as a guiding light.
In its essence, detached involvement is about taking full responsibility for how you're showing up to a situation by getting clear
on what *is* yours to worry about and what *isn't*. When someone is
too attached to an outcome, they become myopic and grippy. The
blinders are put on and they lose sight of perspective or other

avenues they could take to the same exact outcome. Essentially, they become attached. This can manifest as neediness (in my case with my husband's sobriety), obsession, or lack of clarity.

Detached involvement, on the other hand, offers a new opportunity for engagement. This approach allows one to be completely involved in the process, the people, the possibilities of what they want—but ultimately detached to the outcome. There is an undertone of faith in this term. Basically, do your part and your work and release the attachment to what transpires. The concept, which I think of as being cousins with losing ambition, has helped hundreds of our clients, and, blessedly, it helped me when I needed it most in unhooking myself from the journey of others—even the one closest to me.

How does this story end? The work of staying on our own journeys has brought us closer than ever before on our shared one. And, yes, like anything else worthwhile—our health, our careers, our friendships—it requires conscious time and attention. During our second date, over a steak and a bottle (or two) of Stag's Leap Artemis, we both knew that this was the person we would build a life with. Our love didn't start as a head-over-heels, madly in love kind of love. It started as an unquestionable, solid kind of love where we decided that night that we would move out of northern NJ and into Manhattan together. We bought a New York City apartment a few months later on Valentine's Day—before we were even engaged. That night, we could both see the partner with whom we wanted to experience all of the joys and chaos of life. Through the years, we have certainly overanalyzed the smallest decisions in our lives, but the big ones have continued to come effortlessly and intuitively.

How can you stay committed to your (re)evolution?

Somehow, by unraveling the culturally-inherited need to be in control of one another's journey, we have learned to grow and trust our shared one in sublime ways.

. . .

I want to pause and prompt you into a bit of reflective space to consider where you have spent time and energy postponing your own unraveling in order to support that of another. It might be a sibling, an aging parent, a sick child, a job—something that has superseded your own intentionality and growth. There is no blame or judgment here, but as a fellow traveler, I urge you to embrace the power of detached involvement and staying on your own journey. How can you stay committed to your (re)evolution while detaching from the outcomes and influences of others' paths? This is not a call towards isolation. It merely gives you the gift of solitude so you can identify what is yours and what needs to be retired or returned to its source on the unraveling path. Only then can you re-emerge whole, complete, and ready to shine your light in a world that desperately needs it.

7
SPEAK YOUR TRUTH

HOW DO YOU feel when someone's first question to you is, "What do you do?"

I really don't like the question. It stirs up a lot of ambition's shadows for me. Whether I'm at a networking event or just walking the dog, the question feels jarring—intrusive, almost. Even after all of these years of coaching people to own their own power, I believe this question has triggered stress and imposter syndrome in humans for decades. The question is latent with judgment. Once you answer, the other person is filing it away in their mental rolodex (I'm dating myself, I know) to begin assessing if they like you, if you're smart enough, if your profession is acceptable, if you make decent money, and so on. The question is infested with an unintentional but nonetheless potent judgment stemming from ambition, with its focus on what you've done with your life thus far (and whether or not it's "worthy").

My answer to this question definitely reflects the understated, people-pleasing side of me. While I have an objectively impressive resume and believe I do very meaningful work in this world, you would never know this by my often wilting answer: "I'm a coach" or "I teach leaders" or "I work in the leadership development space." My husband cringes when he hears me. He implores—sometimes silently, with a look, and other times out loud in front of the other person—"Why don't you share what you *actually* do, the incredible clients you work with, and how you change them and their businesses?"

We all worked at warp speeds with busy-ness as our culturally accepted scorecard.

The truth is, I don't know why I'm not more honest with this question. I shrink so that I don't make others feel less than. I dim my light so that I can read the audience first and ensure we have traction. Old people-pleasing habits die hard, I know. I exhibit the same behavior on a stage. I can razzle and dazzle any audience* and completely skip the part where I talk about myself, my business—even when it's obvious that there is a moment to "sell" myself. I'm still unlearning and reprogramming.

I wonder if the true question that is really begging to be asked beneath the surface of "What do you do?" is "Hey, can you tell me a bit about who you are and what matters to you right now?" Sometimes, there is so much complexity in the latter that perhaps it's just easier to file people in a mental compartment of *Job Title, Company*. Prior to 2020, I might have lost the battle of trying to change the way people engage with this question. We all worked at warp speeds with busy-ness as our culturally accepted score-card. We read the articles about the cost of busy-ness, found them

---

* With one notable exception: I *did* volunteer to do a talk for the fifth graders at my beloved elementary school. This was by far my toughest audience to date due to a shockingly low attention span. They were poking holes in their paper tablecloths with pencils and spinning around in their chairs while I attempted to teach them about identifying their strengths. . . I neither razzled nor dazzled them.

interesting for about a minute, and reverted back to a predictable pace. We loved this part of the ambition train, even if we claimed to loathe it. Being busy made us feel important, like we mattered. Juggling a lot was an indicator of a rich and full life, despite the cost behind the scenes.

In the post-pandemic era and as we continue to recover, however, I believe the game is forever changed. At first, the stats were looking promising. Productivity, revenue, and growth were through the roof by the end of 2020 for most of our tech clients. Employees could tackle their work at all hours, including resurrected commuting hours, and maximize their input and output in remote locations around the world. Increasing numbers of geographically dispersed teams offered the chance to share more work and pass the baton across time zones to get more products shipped and more programs delivered. Work provided a way to feel control, purpose, and even normalcy in a world that was slipping through our collective fingertips. A welcome distraction from a breaking world, no?

Not so much. The first alarming indicators were tales of sheer exhaustion. Clients tried the obvious strategies—a day off, limited technology before bed, eating at a regular cadence. A few months later, the normal tools and techniques to tackle burnout were null and void. Much like the virus, the burnout had mutated. It felt different and sounded different. People began to resign from jobs they once loved, uprooting their families to move across the world to be closer to family and friends. Managers and HR departments called us at staggering rates to help them navigate the trending exodus. We engaged in several listening tours to really understand this variant of burnout, its root causes, and its side effects.

Here is what we discovered: loneliness and lack of safety were suffocating people. No one could iterate these words exactly, but our excavation revealed the rot eating away at people's previously secure foundations and their understanding of where and how they fit into the world.

- Heaps of employees had onboarded remotely, which prevented company culture from taking root—the lunch table, the chat with a new colleague, the welcome hug from a manager, and the team dinner to formally greet the new joiners were now obsolete.
- Teams (even normally geographically distant teams) that were used to coming together on a weekly, monthly, or even annual basis were stuck behind screens trying to navigate tough conversations and advance trust-building activities with little traction.
- Sheer momentum of scale propelled individual contributors into management roles for the first time without giving them tools, training, or resources. These newly minted managers replaced celebratory career progress with a feeling of drowning and falling behind. The stress was exacerbated by the emotional weight of caring for direct reports without even knowing how to care for themselves.
- Employees became servants to their calendars. Meetings started on the hour, every hour, causing (an expected) chronic lateness to every meeting coupled with an inability to incorporate basic self-care like eating, breaking, and even using the restroom.
- The world of social justice (or rather, lack thereof) imploded, leaving employees panicked about how to engage in new and different ways. They froze in mass confusion, not knowing what to say, what not to say, how to learn, and how to unlearn.
- Family time that was once sacred morphed into abrupt interruptions, unexpected remote school demands, and

distracted work time. Whether employees were caring for a teenager, a newborn, a roommate, a pet, or a plant—the bedroom door was not enough of a buffer.

It's needless to state the collective heaviness of lives scorched by health scares and the tragic loss of those both near and far.

What we discovered wasn't necessarily always a *literal* loneliness (although it was for some). For most of our clients and teams, the loneliness was deeper and more existential in nature. It was feeling lonely within ourselves—wanting to regain a sense of purpose, meaning, and control. Externally, there was a longing for camaraderie, culture, connection. This was a case of human beings wanting desperately to be seen. Humans yearning to remember who they are and to muster up the courage to find themselves once again, even in the messiness of the recovering pandemic era.

We have all heard the buzzwords attempting to capture this existential phenomenon over the past few years—The Great Resignation, Employee Exodus, Quiet Quitting, The Great Regret, The Great Rehiring, and, recently, "rebalancing layoffs of hyper-resourced companies." We have faced collective dissatisfaction and are desperate to do something about it. Call me an optimist, but I believe that these uneasy times are nothing to fear. This season of reckoning is a very important reset. It is tilling the fertile soil of change, growth, and authentic foundation-setting. It is an opportunity to stop compartmentalizing our lives into "personal" and "professional." It's a season of integration. It's a chance to reclaim the personal leadership that naturally resides at the heart of each and every one of our lives.

> Feeling lonely within ourselves—wanting to regain a sense of purpose, meaning, and control.

Rather than a habit of asking "What do you do?" I want to collectively invite us to instead answer the unasked questions of "Who are you and what matters to you, to your team, or your organization right now?" Rather than a world of linear and logical progression, we have an opportunity for quantum leaps in connecting with ourselves and one another. Rather than a world graded by busy-ness, we get a moment to pause and sit with who we are right now. We've changed—we can't go back to our former shape. It's time to choose to respond rather than react. And this pregnant moment, I believe, is the necessary spark for inviting in true personal leadership.

I've learned over and over again through countless client interactions that people don't change unless one of two things happen: joy or pain. We either wire ourselves towards extreme joy when thinking about a potential future state (when we have lost the weight or moved to that city or started that company or taken the trip) or we wire ourselves to avoid pain (fear of the illness due to the weight, fear of regret if we don't move or build or travel).

Sadly, because we have such infrequent glimpses of being able to hold joy for sustained periods of time, we are less comfortable changing for joy. As a result, this space between joy and pain becomes our comfort zone. It's perpetually and suffocatingly comfortable. We stay there for days, weeks, years, even lifetimes. Recall my optimism now. Because we have faced fear like never before as a collective, there is a window for real change here—evolution, actually. There is an opportunity to use that fear to redefine how we experience ourselves, our lives, and one another.

I believe that one of the best gifts we can give one another and this bizarre post-pandemic world is the power of our listening. Quick leadership lesson; grab your notebook. There are several types of listening and they are not all created equal. Most people listen to rebut or refute. They are literally hearing the words come out of the other person's mouth but their brain is processing their response, their next move, the various ways to poke holes in a perspective. This is why so much pain is often harbored in work dynamics that quickly erode trust. Companies proudly claim "debate," or its more tech-friendly cousin, "sparring," is the best way to engage with one another, but unfortunately, without proper parameters, this results in a defensive type of listening that actually creates distance between the parties involved.

Some more evolved listeners listen to engage. They like to chime in—about themselves. You know those friends and colleagues? We all have them. You pour out your heart or share a story about your recent challenge only for them to tell you how they had exactly the same (or juicier) experience. This is a type of listening that masquerades as empathy because the listener tells him- or herself that they don't want the speaker to feel alone so they share a similar experience to make the listener feel more comfortable. These good-intentioned listeners end up chiming in with their own experience and taking the spotlight away from the speaker, leaving them feeling unheard and unacknowledged. This type of listening causes a lot of spinning and wasted energy in the business world, as well as in friendships and family relationships.

For those of you who love to chime in with personal stories, don't despair! I know your intentions are pure and good. The best way to hold space for the other party is to name your connection and then turn the microphone back to them. Say something like: "Wow—I had such a similar experience. I'll share that with you later—please keep going." This allows you to blurt out your enthusiasm of connection without stealing the spotlight. Try it; I promise it will open the window for a deeper type of connection.

Once you start to really watch for these two types of listening, you'll find them to be omnipresent. My husband and I laugh about it all the time. We call one father to say hello and get a laundry list of to-dos that he needs help with, a frantic panic of getting locked out of his websites (because he typed in the wrong password. . . again), and explicit instructions that we should hurry up to have another child—all with that friendly reminder to save 20% of what we earn. He listens to speak and vent. We call the other father to say hello and get asked what we had for dinner. Before finishing the sentence, we are reminded as to why his version of lamb and potatoes is the best, as well as which seasonings he used not only for dinner last night but also for lunch and breakfast earlier that day. He listens to share and talk. Both well-intentioned, both offer repetitive comic relief, *and* we can learn from them about how to move into a more dynamic and collaborative form of listening.

I believe that truly empathetic listening without an agenda is a gift of love.

Lastly, there is a small minority of listeners who practice the craft really well. These listeners are both hearing and listening and are doing this in service to the speaker. In the spirit of true empathy, these listeners acknowledge and validate first. They allow space and silence so that the speaker really feels heard (a most precious gift). They might even follow up with a question to probe deeper rather than making a statement. These listeners can change the world—and certainly their families, communities, and organizations. When people feel heard, energy moves. When people feel seen, they muster up newly discovered reserves of courage to make empowered decisions and move their life in new directions. It's a beautiful thing to witness and experience. I believe that truly empathetic listening without an agenda is a gift of love.

By offering this generous form of listening to one another, we actually start hearing *ourselves* more clearly, too. We see how someone responds when we share a bit of ourselves without interruption. We find a bit more courage when we are asked, "What do you do?" rather than jumping to, "I run a leadership development company."

Perhaps instead you breathe, soften, and share something closer to the heart. "I'm really passionate about helping people find the place where business and spirituality intersect. We spend so much time at work, I've dedicated this chapter of my life to helping find new ways of being, connecting, and working. I'm writing about it right now in my new book—and also spending some of my time teaching and building retreats for leaders so they can do the same for their organizations. Oh, and anytime I'm not doing this, I'm negotiating with a toddler on how quickly she can put on PJs, attempt to go potty, or get into the carseat now that everything is about claiming her freedom."

Ah, now that feels better. Your turn.

8
LOVE (AS A VERB)

THE TOPIC OF love requires another book—or library, even. Love might even seem like a strange topic on an otherwise intense journey of unraveling, especially given that we've been on a roll diving into some personal leadership tips, tools, and concepts. However, I believe any story of unraveling and losing ambition would be incomplete without a brief rest stop here. Love transcends. It helps us slow down and zoom out to a less chaotic space

> Love is most potently experienced when activated as a practice.

so we can assess where we are on our journey thus far. I have learned so much about love during this past decade of personal leadership and self-actualization. Allow me to share a few nuggets that I hope will be useful to you.

First and foremost, I've learned that, while love takes many forms and can be found at many different altitudes, it is most potently experienced when activated as a practice. Let's take gratitude, for example. Gratitude is a very effective portal into love. Sadly, it is usually engaged conceptually rather than truly practiced. You can't post #grateful on your social media and experience the fullness of the love behind it. I've worked with gratitude lists for as long as I can remember. Sometimes I can feel the charge of love, and, other times, it's purely an intellectual experience or feels like something I "should" do.

One of the best hacks I've discovered that helps up the ante on gratitude is to add the word "because" after I think about or write out the thing for which I'm grateful. It's very different to say "I'm grateful for my dog Henry today," versus "I'm grateful for my dog Henry because he just warmed up the bed and my toes were freezing." "Because" unlocks the present moment as an opportunity to really draw in the energy of what you are appreciating about the person or thing. Try it.

One level deeper, I've discovered that love lives in the shift between sympathy and empathy. Often confused as synonymous, there is a world of a difference between the two. Sympathy is feeling someone's feelings for them—the pain, the regret, the worry. You feel "bad" for them or can sympathize with their experience because you've been in their shoes. (Notice how similar sympathy feels to that level of listening where you are only listening to chime in.)

Sympathy typifies a very Greek type of love. We feel so deeply for those around us that we actually pride ourselves on making that pain our own. My parents would often proclaim, "When you are happy, we are 100 times happier. When you are sad, we are 100 times sadder." No pressure.

That sympathetic type of love can suffocate. Rather than just one of us going through something tough with the rest strong and ready to support on the sidelines, we're now all going through something tough with no one to help pull us out. Sympathy can create distance if you listen between the lines: *I'm so sorry you're going through that—and I'm relieved it's not me.*

Empathy, on the other hand, is holding space for the other person to feel their feelings and their own unique experience. Empathy allows us to see the other person in their wholeness, even if they are temporarily experiencing suffering or hardship. Empathy is a way of staying on your own journey while helping others know that they are not alone. Empathetic love fosters resilience in others, so they can discover the wellspring of resources within themselves.

A great coaching tool for accessing empathy is called "normalizing." Rather than chiming in with your experience or a resource or a solution straight away, normalizing is about steadfast reassurance. You let the other person know that what they are feeling or experiencing is completely normal and anyone in their shoes would feel the same way. Moreover, they are allowed to have their feelings and feel them fully.

We often complain to our loved ones, "I just want you to listen—I don't want you to problem-solve!" That's a surefire sign that you're in sympathy mode. The pain was uncomfortable enough for *you* that it was time to solve it for the other person. Empathy can create connections if you listen between the lines. *You are going through so much right now. Anyone in your shoes would feel this overwhelm. I'm not going anywhere—tell me more.*

> Self-love is the fuel that makes transformation possible.

An examination of love would not be complete without pausing for a moment to dissect self-love. Here's what I've learned so far, and it is as profound as it sounds: self-love is the fuel that makes transformation possible. You can transform aspects of yourself, learn new habits, find new friends, move apartments, change jobs—but without loving yourself, you will eventually return to the same feelings of all-consuming existential emptiness.

As I really started to understand the inner workings of empathy (not just as a tool in my coaching kit), I was intrigued to find that empathy towards myself unlocked more love in my life. A few years back, I took a spiritual course on the ascension of human consciousness. (Yes, this is my idea of fun.) The instructor designed the entire semester around an understanding of love being the only thing we need to master in this lifetime. She approached it from all angles—how to use love to accept change and discover resilience within ourselves, how to anchor ourselves in love to feel more safe during turmoil, how to connect to higher frequencies of energy and healing through love. I was following along (like a good student) intellectually and doing all of the reading and meditations, but I didn't quite get the gravitas of the love she was describing until one of the Q&As. A fellow student asked her to expand on imposter syndrome and why we're all perpetually hard on ourselves no matter our level of success, achievement, and perceived happiness (hello again, ambition!).

The instructor replied with a lesson I will never forget and feel grateful to be able to share with you. She explained that imposter syndrome stems from a lack of self-love (or self-empathy, self-kindness, self-care). It is something we train ourselves to experience (back to forgetting who we are the first half of our lives!). We forget our wholeness as an integral part of the human web. We forget our divinity and sacred connection to all there is. We forget that all of the power, abundance, and joy in the world resides within us. Without self-love, we cut off access to this inherent birthright. She continued to share that low self-esteem, imposter syndrome, mental chatter—whatever you want to call it—is essentially the accumulation of all the moments when we abandon ourselves.

Abandoning ourselves.
Abandoning myself.
I've abandoned myself.
Whoa.
Wait—that's the punchline of this whole season of unraveling!
Whoa.
Blind ambition is my form of abandoning myself.
Whoa.
I've spent four decades abandoning myself.
Whoa.

The words reverberated throughout my entire being, like they can only do when you know you've stumbled across one of your life's truths.

Before this course, I was well-versed in the concept of an inner child and healing past trauma. I knew my imposter syndrome tools inside-out and had helped countless clients find strength to persevere beyond the hold of the feeling that they were an imposter—remember, I teach what I need to learn most for a living. Until that moment, though, I had never truly understood the incessant humming of feeling low self-worth as a *side effect* of perpetual acts of self-abandonment. Imposter syndrome wasn't the root cause, as I had falsely believed it to be all this time. Imposter syndrome was the *side effect* of the root cause: self-abandonment.

> Imposter syndrome was the *side effect* of the root cause: self-abandonment.

Self-abandonment was my former responsible, good-girl fix and success strategy—contorting myself and my needs to what the world around me required so I could ensure harmony and esteem. Help others, people-please, over-rotate on imbalanced responsibility. While I was very familiar with the behavior of ignoring my needs, I had never heard it phrased as self-abandonment. The thing I feared the most (abandonment), the thing I set my entire life up to avoid (abandonment), the thing I staged ambition to counteract (abandonment), was the very crime I was committing to my own heart each day.

So, how did I start to reclaim those forgotten pieces? How do you begin to reclaim yours?

That's right—it's a disciplined practice. I committed to trying self-love on for size. I vowed to act in alignment with what I felt and needed, consistently and in perpetuity. The vow holds true for the simple things and the profound. Once I committed, I saw the transgressions everywhere. I mean, everywhere.

When my husband asks if I want to go to a Mexican or French restaurant for dinner and I choose Mexican to make him happy because I can sense his preference (but I don't like Mexican food because cilantro is my culinary nemesis), this is a moment of self-abandonment. When a friend wants to chat and complain for the hundredth time about the same things and I say "yes," even though I had scheduled an hour to myself, this is a moment of self-abandonment. When I play Switzerland during a family feud, rather than offer the strong opinion I have, because I don't want to upset anyone, this is a moment of self-abandonment. When I am exhausted and need a nap, but instead decide to do laundry or clean up Emilia's pink plastic toys for the tenth time that day, this is a moment of self-abandonment. When I decide to check email for a few hours rather than write a chapter of this book that is so important to me, this is a moment of self-abandonment.

I was reminded about how my friends growing up thought it was very weird that I would enjoy watching movies by myself or taking myself and a book out to lunch. (This was before the now commonplace understanding of the concepts of introversion and extroversion as energy preferences.) I feel so sad for that girl that tossed aside what she really needed (time to recharge her batteries in an authentic and empowering way) and chose likability instead. The moments are endless; I had crafted a life of self-abandonment which was sneakily camouflaged as ambition, being helpful, fixing problems, being productive—perfection.

Stop for a moment and check in with yourself, engaging in some steadfast honesty. Where do you notice these micro-moments of transgression? How do you feel after you've said "yes" when you meant to say "no?" How do you shake off your disappointment when you've silenced your preference. . . again? There is no need to blame or shame here—that only perpetuates the damage. This is a moment of neutral observation sprinkled with self-love and kindness.

> The opportunities to repair are plenty, and I have promised myself that I will put in a Valia-nt effort.

I know that I have a lot of damage control to do with myself—and that it will be a lifelong journey of repair. This book is an act of self-love. Taking time to meditate and pray, move my body, and journal my emotions are all acts of self-love. Pausing before saying a habitual "yes" is an act of self-love. Learning to see and set boundaries as keeping myself in (versus keeping others out) is an act of self-love. Getting off a client call on time rather than going over (again) and calling it generosity is an act of self-love. Eating lunch without rushing or losing myself on Instagram is an act of self-love. The opportunities to repair are plenty, and I have promised myself that I will put in a Valia-nt effort.

· · ·

I am unapologetic about my love of quotes. From the moment I could write (yes—on that chalkboard), I would capture inspirational sayings, words, concepts, and quotes. Growing up, my room was littered with cheesy quotes on those wooden signs. *Peace. Love. Harmony. Seize the day.* My journals to this day are a collection of my scavenger hunt for words that inspire and move me.

Early in my coaching career, I applied to a very prestigious global leadership development firm. Part of our interview process was delivering a sample workshop in front of the partners of the firm. I started off my interview presentation with a quote that was truly perfect for the occasion (or so I thought). Although I was quite young and inexperienced in the coaching craft at the time, the partners saw potential and moved me to the next rounds of interviews and eventually onboarded me into the firm. I wove quotes into my presentations and materials where relevant in order to have the audience pause and reflect on the topic before we dove in. One of the senior partners pulled me aside after a program one day and gave me direct feedback (the firm prided itself on this). "Valia, you've got to stop with the quotes. This is not what leaders are looking for."

I was embarrassed—my passion had intruded on my professional persona. I dropped the quotes and played the game by their rules. My people-pleaser instincts knew what to do and I jumped into full ambition gear—impressing them, ever the good student, delivering the programs exactly how they wanted.

A few years later, I was invited to join the core faculty for one of the firm's most important clients, a top global consulting firm. It was a five-day intensive program focused on the soft skills of leadership and would be delivered throughout the world, several times a year. As we settled down for our program onboarding, the client took out a packet of five-by-nine inch pieces of paper and shared that this was to be the anchor of the program for all the work we would do throughout those five days. I opened the packet only to literally laugh out loud. The packet contained about thirty inspirational quotes from famous figures throughout the world. Quotes on leadership, hardship, resilience, hope, love. The quotes were our entry into the program—participants would walk around the room in a simulated "gallery walk" to read them and be inspired by the various leaders. From there, participants would discuss the shared values they saw across the room and make connections between leadership and values. Later on in the program, they would have the opportunity to define their own values and how they see the world.

I led that client and those teams for several years because the work was so meaningful to me and aligned with my truth. This was a place where I could explicitly help people make connections between language and values, listening and trust, courage and compassion. That early work informed a lot of my approach for *The Paradox of Leadership* today, and every time I put a quote in one of our presentations, I smile and remember the power of self-love. I knew those quotes back in that interview process were critical to building leadership culture. The partners just hadn't seen it quite yet.

There was another moment of self-love and trust that bubbles to the top of my mind when I need to be courageous and stand for what I know is right. It was early days in my solo practice and I had joined a few coaching "houses" to get more exposure and hone my craft. These coaching houses represented hundreds of coaches and would match coaches with executive clients in their network while taking a portion of the engagement fees in exchange. It was a great way to learn and onboard into the industry.

One of the first steps was to nail your coaching bio so the "house" could start marketing you to potential clients. I was delighted to have found my life's work and proudly wrote my bio in a way that allowed my authenticity to shine. I talked about my empathy and the ways I could really connect with a client on the inner work of leadership. At some point, I used the word "holistic" in the context that I believe that true leadership is both personal and professional and that my approach to coaching would mirror that belief.

The managing director of the coaching firm reached out to me, saying the bio looked great, but I should drop the word "holistic" because it sounded too "woo-woo" for their audience. My people-pleaser and inner knowingness found themselves in battle. The easy thing would have been to drop the word—two seconds, delete. I would seem agreeable and impress this woman so she could bump my bio to the top of her coach recommendations. My inner knowingness (yes, self-love), however, couldn't look the other way. All of the work that I had done to recover from the panic attacks and collect missing pieces of myself pointed to "holistic" being an integral part of my new, budding profession.

Despite my comfort with accommodating others, this time I decided to stand for what mattered to me. I made an appointment to see her in person and explained that I was hoping to work with the clients who understood the "holistic" language and were actually inspired by it—perhaps tech companies or other progressive industries. She shook her head and said it was my choice, but that, by keeping the word in, my prospects would be very limited with their firm. I accepted.

Fast forward to a chemistry meeting with one of my very first and favorite clients—a senior executive at a global advertising firm. The meeting couldn't have gone better—he opened up and shared about his past, how he got to the firm, what he was hoping to get out of the coaching engagement, and some more personal disclosures. There were tears at some point (I have a pretty high tear statistic, too) and I could see how deeply he wanted to feel seen and appreciated for his contributions.

A few months after he selected me as his coach and our work had begun, we were wrapping up a session and he offered some very thoughtful praise on how much he was enjoying the work and our progress. I couldn't help but ask him what made him choose me over the other coaches. I was clearly young and just starting out. I remember that moment to this day: "Easy. You had the word 'holistic' in your resume. That intrigued me because it was different. And when I met you, I knew you walked the talk. You were the real deal."

Sometimes self-love is sticking with what you know to be true at all costs and making tough choices. Other times, it's just a quiet inner confirmation that you trust the path you're on. What I know for sure, though, is that once you have opened the window to explore your relationship with self-abandonment, you can never unsee it. Thus unravels another thread of the losing ambition journey.

Take a second to breathe here.

Again.

Once more.

What memories are bouncing around in your head and heart right now? Where might you have (knowingly or unknowingly) chosen self-abandonment over self-love? What happened? More importantly, what did you learn? These wounds may sting for a while, but they also hold the antidote for what you are learning to unravel. Let me offer another tool that might help unlock something in your discovery.

One of the signature exercises that we do at *The Paradox of Leadership* for our client team retreats is asking participants to dive into the heart of vulnerability by finishing this sentence as many times as possible in ninety seconds (in front of everyone):

What you can't tell by looking at me is _____.

If you just winced, don't worry. You're not alone. This exercise scares the crap out of people. Then it disarms them. It allows for unfiltered truth, it names things that are important to the individual—both the mega and the mundane. It also allows people to see how connected we really are beyond the surface of our job titles or skin color or resumes or religions. It invites empathy and *philoxenia*—the love of the stranger—to help you see yourself in the other.

> These wounds may sting for a while, but they also hold the antidote for what you are learning to unravel.

I have taken teams that were not on speaking terms to a place of profound healing and trust through the help of this exercise. I have helped managers see the needs of their direct reports in unprecedented ways. I have allowed co-founders to reconnect to their reasons why they started the company to begin with and collaboratively reignite passion and purpose. It's a magic tool in our Paradox toolkit, perhaps *because* I believe it to be an act of self-love.

So, here goes. Here's my quick unfiltered ninety seconds—unedited, captured "live" on a California chilly afternoon of

March 9, 2023, before sending this book to publication. Perhaps a brief homage to claim a few more forgotten parts.

- What you can't tell by looking at me is, my favorite movie of all time is *Dirty Dancing*.
- What you can't tell by looking at me is, I really enjoy building Ikea furniture. For hours sometimes. I find it meditative.
- What you can't tell by looking at me is, I don't cook. And am so grateful I married a man who does.
- What you can't tell by looking at me is, I like to spa. Hard.
- What you can't tell by looking at me is, if I didn't run my company, I'd work at The Container Store. Organization is the way to my heart.
- What you can't tell by looking at me is, my father turns eighty-seven this year and it scares me that he won't be around for much longer.
- What you can't tell by looking at me is, as much as I have longed to become a mother, I never realized how lonely and trapped I would also feel.
- What you can't tell by looking at me is, I regret not having more fun in my life (thus far).
- What you can't tell by looking at me is, I'm really afraid of turbulence. And feel ashamed as I type this right now.
- What you can't tell by looking at me is, I'm scared that forty-two is middle-aged.
- What you can't tell by looking at me is, I often feel alone (even if I'm in a room full of people I'm close to).
- What you can't tell by looking at me is, I feel frustrated that my figure has expanded to a mega-pear since childbirth.
- What you can't tell by looking at me is, I didn't know how much unsteadiness can happen in a marriage when a woman is the primary breadwinner.

- What you can't tell by looking at me is, I want to be the Oprah of the business world and live at the intersection of business and spirituality.

Deep breath. Let's continue.

My team and I model something similar that is true for us in front of the room and then we unleash the task to the audience. It's hard. It's raw. It's frightening. It's true. It's an act of self-love. It's empathy. It's courage. It's leadership. At first, you offer something on the surface and then a little more, and a little more, and a little more, until you've reached something meaningful that's on your heart. At least, for right now.

I believe this is where leadership lives. If we stood in front of the room and just spouted out details about what we had for dinner or how many dogs and cats we have or where we recently went on vacation, the space to connect is small. Everyone would repeat surface answers and lighthearted anecdotes. Instead, we are willing and we model what's possible. Once we allow for some honesty and vulnerability (thank you again, Brené)—the entire leadership game changes.

My favorite definition of psychological safety is this: what matters to me is safe with you.

I think this is what love is all about.

"Psychological safety" is a trendy leadership development term that's been buzzing around our industry for a while. My favorite definition of psychological safety is this: what matters to me is safe with you. I think this is such a beautiful testament to love. Whether you offer your gift of holding space to a parent, a neighbor, a partner, a colleague, a child, or yourself, it matters.

Listening (yes, the truly empathetic kind of listening we explored earlier) and holding sacred what matters to another person (even if that person is *you*) is the most important work we will ever do. And I believe it can change the world.

I'll leave with one last nugget on what I've learned about love through the unraveling process. If your practices of gratitude, vulnerability, courageous choices, or self-love don't do the trick, try forgiveness. If you just sighed or shook your head, anticipating unearthing old wounds will require too much work, I hear you. Nearly all of the personal development books on my bookshelf (and there are *many*) talk about forgiveness as the cornerstone of healing. I would often roll my eyes and skip those chapters, thinking they were irrelevant for the ambitious approach to healing. Almost too easy, perhaps?

One of my teachers illuminated forgiveness in a way that has deeply shifted the way I love. She explained that forgiveness has little to do with me or the other person in the narrative. Huh? Instead, forgiveness is a divine practice, requiring us to trust a higher order, surrender to love, know deep within ourselves that everything we experience occurs with perfect timing and fortitude. In other words, forgiveness is admitting that I don't know it all and—happily—I no longer need to carry it all. It is a one-way ticket out of town for ambition. She

> Replace the words "I forgive" with "I let love live here."

showed me that the path of forgiveness *is* an act of love, an invitation to allow myself to be held by the Universe, trusting that it knows better than me.

This concept of forgiveness as an act of love required something of me: a willingness to name the things that no longer served my path—control, worry, anxiety, fear. If this definition of forgiveness were true, if I could surrender to something deeper within me, then the old grip was not only irrelevant, but a façade that prevented me from tapping into peace. It was within me, quietly waiting for my willingness to allow it in for the healing balm that it was. She taught me to replace the words "I forgive" with "I let love live here."

I discovered that the person I needed to forgive (to let love live here) most of all was me—for being so hard on myself for all of these years (and decades), for holding myself to impossible standards, for taking on the weight of every outcome, relationship, and responsibility, for settling for less than I deserved. Letting love live in these spaces of my history is still a work in progress. It is a daily practice that requires replacing one pattern with a healthier one. It is noticing a moment of disharmony and actively changing my mindset, habit, and behavior. Like an old teacher once shared, "There is nothing sexy about the spiritual path. Each day it feels like chopping wood and carrying water." And so it is.

9
ALLOW THE PARADOX

SINCE WE'RE KNEE-DEEP in existential topics like love and for-giveness, let's sprinkle in one more dimension of the human experience that's noteworthy during unraveling ambition: our relationship to time. I believe that the truest aspects of our lives—love, connection, joy, peace—live beyond our human construct of time. They are universal and forever. I started this year with the ultimate quote (wish?) on my vision board: **What if time were this sacred thing that takes care of us?**

Sacred time, meet my ambition's former motto: being on time is being five minutes early, and being five minutes late is—well, why bother? Go home.

The number of arguments my husband and I have had around time and how we manage it are endless, ranging from the pas-sive aggressive, "Oh, I thought you were going to pick me up at 2 p.m.," to the outright furious, "If you don't show up on time, you have zero respect for us." What for me is a language of consideration, for him is a language of freedom. My good girl insides knew that part of the winning

> What if time were this sacred thing that takes care of us?

formula was showing up early to everything, while his suffocated, first-generation, family business insides were desperate to steal a moment to himself to enjoy and play. I think we've only recently— and gratefully (with a ton of work)—snapped out of our struggles here (thirteen years later!). It took a lot of learning, curiosity, listening, and empathy. *Yes, I get it, I teach what I need to learn most!*

I recall the moment that broke the pattern—it was an epic one. We were heading out to my husband's birthday dinner and he was twenty minutes late to come home and pick me up. I sat on the couch brewing with resentment as I waited. He came in, gave his usually ambivalent apology of "sorry I'm late," and went off to get dressed. I followed him into the room, looked straight into his eyes and said, "I don't get it. Honestly. Did you hear that being on time really matters to me and makes me feel safe?"

He snapped, "It's not like we had an appointment. I'm just picking you up for dinner."

We both shot silent daggers into each other and bit our tongues because the babysitter was in the other room.

As soon as we closed the car doors, we unleashed our "is this going to work?" argument. He threatened to pick up and leave for New York that night. My abandonment alarm was coding red and I made a snide comment about what a great choice it would be to get up and leave his wife and soon-to-be one-year-old. We tossed accusations back and forth like professionals. Then there was silence. We were tired. He had been furloughed for almost two years. I was resentful that all the financial strain of our life was on me again. We had just found our footing after his sobriety journey.

He looked at me in surrender and said, "You know—all of these years, I have never once tried to change you. And all you ever do is try and change me."

I can't remember what I said or if I said anything at all because I was so shocked by his accusation. But I do remember *exactly* how I felt: head-to-toe shame. He was *completely* right. My ambition of turning my husband into the exact version of him that made me feel safe drowned out any possibility of real empathy for and understanding of him. I had spent over a decade fixing, coaching, urging, motivating, recommending, reminding, mothering. It was time to accept him exactly as he was—the "late" parts and all—or start packing up and saying goodbye.

I share this story because while being on time or not seems like such an innocuous thing to be putting strain on a relationship, it's not. Our relationship to time (or money, education, or any other ways we measure ourselves against the world) is embedded in our identity. From the moment I could show up places on my own, I prided myself on being early—all the time, no exception. It made me feel like a true "good girl." It fueled my fragile self-esteem when I was complimented for being responsible. Having to unlearn my dependency on being on time was a significant leg of my ambition-losing journey. In a way, they seemed one in the same.

A leadership concept that was fundamental to my own healing around time and our foundation-building work with clients around resilience is the difference between *energy* and *time.* We have all been indoctrinated to master the management of our time—tools, resources, apps, calendars abound. However, we haven't been exposed until recently to the generative possibilities of managing energy. Time, at least in our 3D world, is a depleting resource. It is always shrinking and there is never enough of it to do and experience all we want (thus perpetuating people like yours truly feeling like they are never enough). Energy, on the other hand, is a resource that can be manipulated. We can create it, generate more of it, amplify it, even transmute it. To master the quality and quantity of our energy is a big shortcut in unraveling ambition.

In my early days of building a coaching business in New York City, my calendar was a magical Tetris game. I was a traveling circus from the moment I left my house in the morning to the moment I returned late in the evening after wrapping up a networking or speaking event. I would go from office to office to subway to bus to taxi to uptown to downtown to crosstown. I would make plans for each location in accordance with time of day, the traffic on the subway, and the proximity to restrooms and my favorite coffee shops for a quick break between clients. I would layer in considerations of weather and how many literal layers I would have to lug around all day, the time of year—with tourists if I was venturing near midtown Manhattan—, and possible pauses for a stroll with a friend or a potential new partner.

On Sunday evenings, the calendar was locked and loaded—perfected and ready for the week ahead. Life, being real life, and me, being in a professional service industry, made it so that I would have to deal with appointments being rescheduled, clients getting sick, and locations changing at the last minute. These schedule changes would irk me at first and later truly test my patience during my building-a-business marathon years. I would regularly complain to my coach about how I felt my time was being wasted and my energy being disrespected. Every canceled appointment felt like a deprioritization of me and a personal attack on the calendar I had so lovingly and meticulously crafted to make all the magic happen.

My wonderful coach offered me a tool that I still use to this day and teach clients to build for themselves. It is the epitome of the difference between solving for time versus solving for energy.

First off, she helped me shift my mindset (as all good coaches do) and consider a canceled appointment as a gift of time returned back to me. From there, she encouraged me to build an energy list. Essentially, her question was: *What would I do with a gift of time in the increments of five minutes, fifteen minutes, thirty minutes, one hour, a half-day, and even a day?* She asked me to list the items that would energize me in each of those time segments and across several energy parameters—physical, mental, emotional, spiritual. After the lists were complete, the instructions were clear: *If someone cancels an appointment, don't go into frustration. Don't check your email. Take out the piece of paper and choose one item on the list in the appropriate time bracket.*

It was the permission I needed to start honoring myself, my time, *and* my energy, and stop feeling like a victim to other people's time choices. It was an act of self-love. Rather than get annoyed that the client was running fifteen minutes late, I would take out my phone and look at photos and videos of our Boston Terrier, Henry, to make me laugh. Rather than pout about commuting one hour to downtown Manhattan only to find out the client was called into an emergency meeting and needed to reschedule, I found my way to the 9/11 museum to sit with a piece of New York City's heart. Rather than roll my proverbial eyes that the same client needed to end early for the third session in a row, I would delight in a few moments of sunshine and book-reading on their rooftop terrace.

• • •

Stop for a moment and consider all of the ways you believe your time to be "wasted." Your commute, waiting in a school pick-up line, kids getting sick and needing to cancel your day, a long airplane ride, a friend canceling your coffee date at the last minute, traffic. What if, instead of "waste," you saw these moments as true gifts? What if these were tiny moments of self-love you could use to reconnect with yourself, take a breath, and recommit to the rest of your day? What if the universe were consciously opening up some space in your life—just for you?

By now, it probably won't surprise you to learn that I am a woman of synchronicity, not coincidence. I believe that everything happens in divine and perfect time and the more we trust this universal current, the more in flow our lives become. It was only when I was able to move beyond the confines of my dependency on literal time—*chronos*, in Greek—that I was able to start experiencing the real magic of a more divine and mythic time, known as *kairos*. The more I let go of my addiction to controlling time (in huge part thanks to my lesson from my husband and being reminded to stay on my own journey once again), the more the synchronicities revealed themselves.

> What if the universe were consciously opening up some space in your life—just for you?

There were the obvious reminders to trust divine timing—thinking of someone and having the phone ring a second later; reading the exact quote that gets mentioned by a client the next day; wanting to send a gift to a friend to find the exact gift at my doorstep.

Then there were magical ones, the kind that move you to tears and confirm once and for all how magical this life really is.

My mother decided to recently (and suddenly) sell my childhood home in northern New Jersey. After over forty years, she insisted the house was too large and her aging body and mind were calling for smaller spaces and less "stuff." The move was chaotic and rushed. What we thought would take months to sell turned into a competitive cash offer that required my parents to clear their entire life in less than thirty days. I flew home and went into extreme program management mode for just five days: donation boxes, Craigslist piles to sell, 1-800-Got-Junk? for piles and fixtures that were impossible to sell, boxes to ship to Greece, movers arranged for other boxes to ship to California (where my husband and I now lived), setting up storage units in NJ in case they wanted to return. It was utter stress and we had no other choice—the decision was made.

It was impossible to savor the luxury of nostalgia in five short days, so I threw out most of my childhood memories—furniture, toys, books—and packed a couple of boxes with special items to send back to California. When the boxes labeled "Valia's memorabilia" arrived a few weeks later, I decided to do another quick clearing so we could at least keep the storage unit organized and reclaim our sanity after a wild move.

There were sweet memories and mementos in these boxes. Old letters to friends, photo IDs from high school and college, ticket stubs, old diaries, cassette tapes (yes, '80s), special photographs. A big padded envelope said "wedding" and I paused to look through it. In the folder were wedding venue papers and contracts, magazine scraps of inspiration for the flowers and favors. I found the receipt for my wedding dress that my mom must have slipped into the folder with the other clippings. I blinked a few times to reread the word and make sure I wasn't mistaken. My wedding gown—purchased twelve years prior and completely unbeknownst to me—was named "Emilia."

All is always okay, taken care of, divinely orchestrated.

You've already learned how organically we chose my daughter Emilia's name during the embryo phases of IVF. I couldn't believe it. Goosebumps jolted down my entire spine, tears streamed down my face, I looked up, and said, *Thank you, Universe.* Thank you for showing me that all is always okay, taken care of, divinely orchestrated.

It's so fascinating how life makes little sense as we're living through it, but makes perfect sense when we look back and see all the clues and lessons for what they were—little guideposts, course-corrections, and winks along our journey. Truly, what is time in its purest essence if not this divine thing that just takes care of us? That is what I believe and know time to be when we let it—a divine portal into our experiences here on earth.

Releasing the shackles of my former relationship with time has also allowed for a new way to hold seemingly disparate things. Thank you, paradox, you never cease to amaze me. Let me explain. Before unraveling my ambition, I had a very linear and literal perception of what filled the moments and days of our lives. First we do the thing, and then we achieve or accomplish the next thing. After that thing, we graduate to this new thing, where we can share many things with these other people. From there, we co-create other things and then let go of some original things and on goes the step-by-step instruction manual for our linear progression through time. There are good times followed by struggles. There are seasons of joy and seasons of sadness. One foot in front of the other, step by step.

One of the most liberating realizations of my ambition journey is that I finally started to hold multiple realities all at once—without having to change anything about them or judge them in any way. I could be surrounded by people *and* feel completely alone. I could be at the peak of ambition's success *and* still feel unworthy. I could be staring right into the eyes of a miracle *and* still find myself consumed by anger, fear, or regret. On the flip side, I could be in the grip of an emergency *and* still experience peace. I could be in a season of loss *and* still find joy and laughter. I could be in the heat of an argu-ment *and* still tap into love and forgiveness.

> When we allow and accept rather than struggle and resist, life moves through us at its own beautiful cadence.

This was an entirely new way of making sense of the world in my brain. Rather than the requisite seasons of joy and seasons of sadness, years of stress and years of abundance, days of flow and days of frustration, time collapsed. In the same day, hour, even moment, I could hold two energies and know that they were both true at the same time. I could be tired *and* find energy to be with my daughter. I could see my point of view *and* my husband's simultaneously. Quietly but assuredly, judgment faded into the background and all of my tools—curiosity, empathy, listening, vul-nerability, detached involvement—started taking center stage. My presence was the key to experiencing it all, at the same time. When we allow and accept rather than struggle and resist, life moves through us at its own beautiful cadence.

The most vivid experience I've had of knowing that both things can be true at once was the passing of my mother-in-law. We found out she had cancer the same week we found out that our IVF procedure was successful and that we were pregnant with Emilia. I would call her each week with updates and send pho-tos of sonograms and she would let us know about her recent procedures and hospital visits. I watched my husband prepare to become a father and prepare to lose his mother in the same sliver of time. We knew we were saying goodbye the Christmas before she passed and all she wanted to do was sing Greek nursery rhymes with the baby. Dread and joy lived in the same few seconds—seemingly incompatible, yet imperfectly perfect companions. After her passing, we found hope and laughter in the signs she would send us (usually a dragonfly) while we would cry for hours at night at the realization that Emilia would never know her grandmother (at least not in this physical plane).

My husband, God bless him, is the morning person in our family unit. He sings Emilia out of bed, sets her up with breakfast, and gets her day started. Right after his mother's passing, Emilia (one year old at the time) would look at her grandma's photo and cheer "Yiayia!" and give her kisses. One day, my husband started asking her if she *sees* Yiayia. She nodded and said "yes" as if he were asking her if the sky is blue. He continued, asking her where Yiayia is. She answered, "with the Angels" (a word we hadn't taught her yet).

The dialogue has gotten more robust over time.

"What did you do with Yiayia last night?" he ponders.
"Painting," she replies, again unfazed.
"What color did you paint with?"
"Purple," she confirms.

My mother-in-law's favorite color was purple, which is something Emilia would have never known but obviously *knew* wholeheartedly.

Thus, I know beyond the shadow of a doubt that linear time is something that keeps us company on this earth journey of which we're all a part. If we dare to look a bit beyond the day-to-day, if we are willing to hold two seemingly disparate things together, if we are brave enough to face the paradox, we see that of course both things are true. Time is depleting *and* it doesn't really exist. Love transcends space and time. Our collective consciousness is evolving to unimaginable places once we traverse through the seeming chaos of our current day.

I realize that unraveling our shared understanding of linear time requires a significant leap of faith—or rather, leap of trust. It is asking you (and me) to trust in new and significant ways while keeping our feet firmly planted on the ground. It asks us to hold two seemingly contradictory energies or experiences at the same time while acknowledging that both are valid and true. It pleads with us to believe in a great unfolding of the sequencing and quantum leaps in our lives. Perhaps it even asks for a little bit of humor and levity—knowing that it is *always*, in *all ways*, okay.

10
ACT AS IF

A SECRET WORLD has always existed in my lineage. As I shared earlier, Greeks, like many other cultures, orient their lives around the infamous evil eye. From the moment a baby is born, you adorn them with blue evil eye charms to ward off the bad spirits—sometimes otherworldly spirits, other times just the jealous lady down the street. I remember, growing up, every time I tasted joy, celebration, happiness, I would quickly be reminded not to harp on it so as to activate the evil eye. Basically, the boogeyman and thief of joy. Every time there was an extra drop of contentment, we waited for the other shoe to drop. Sometimes it did, sometimes it didn't, but the anticipation was enough to dampen my ever feeling safe around happiness.

If the other shoe *did* drop (someone caught a cold, the faucet started leaking, a freak accident occurred), we would activate the chain of command to neutralize and expel the evil eye. My mother would call my grandmother in her small village in the Peloponnese and ask her to begin "the process." Yiayia would run to her kitchen and take out the metallic bronze bowl and fill it with the anointed water. She would then add a few drops of olive oil and, depending on the shape that the oil and water combination made, we were either mildly or gravely under the spell of the evil eye. Funnily enough, we were never just okay. If it was mild, a quick prayer would do. If it was grave, there was a prayer to be repeated several times under my grandmother's breath while we closed our eyes on the other end of the line and asked the evil spirit to leave us. Depending on how much we all yawned and teared, we would know if the spirit had left and how nefarious the spirit was.

After the ritual, we would discuss what we did the day before and who was there to try and target the exact person who initiated the evil—patient zero if you will. *Was it that same woman with the light eyes? She always gets you, doesn't she?! What were you wearing? Be careful next time you talk about school because that other family doesn't go to that school. Keep that news of your piano recital very quiet.* On and on went the list of precautions which were kept until the next time (usually forty-eight to seventy-two hours later). Whether tradition or superstition, we always felt better after we yawned it out and were assured by Yiayia that we were safe to proceed with our day.

On my journey to reclaim the lost parts of myself via unraveling, I discovered that I am (or certainly wish I were) a modern day medicine woman like my grandmother. The humming of this yearning has grown louder through the years. You'll recall the energy tool. Every time there was a substantial amount of time gifted to me (say thirty minutes or more), what I wanted to do most was energize through something in the spiritual bracket. I read blogs from spiritual healers, made appointments for new and interesting therapies, bought tarot cards and learned how to interpret them, discovered sage and crystals. My gifted time became a portal into another world I didn't even know existed for me in the constant noise and drive of my "normal" life—apart from the SOS phone calls to Yiayia.

Looking back, it's clear to me that the world beyond our five senses has always intrigued me. I knew there was meaning beyond the rigidity of Greek Orthodoxy and organized religion in general. There was no way that going to church and sitting through a three-hour mass without understanding a single word was the only answer to finding connection. I began to search quietly. In high school, I loved learning about Native American traditions and the sacred connection to the earth. At Georgetown, I took several courses about witchcraft and became fascinated by those women who could see beyond a literal knowledge of being. I planned a trip with my mom to visit the energy vortexes in Sedona as we took part in several Native American rituals. During summers in Greece, I would lose myself in stargazing and imagining how the universe came to be. I discovered a medium to try and connect with my grandmother after she had

> The world beyond our five senses has always intrigued me.

passed and found tremendous solace in knowing she was okay. I began exploring meditation, yoga, and sound baths before they were on the socially-accepted map. I contorted a corner of our already too-small New York City apartment into a meditation cave, adorned with salt rocks, crystals, sage, and palo santo. Basically, if it felt beyond the obvious and ordinary, I was all in.

During my IVF journey—perhaps as an early act of self love—I gave myself permission to allow this inner world of intrigue to express itself more boldly and explicitly in my daily life. During the COVID lockdown, I trained to become a certified Reiki master to bring energy healing into my uterus, my family, and my work (and, honestly, the world). I now work with several teachers to explore the world of spirit and my place in it. I have integrated the introduction of spiritual concepts and practices into our leadership development programs and have been fascinated by how transformational it has been for clients and their businesses. I am convinced that spiritual leadership is both existential *and* highly practical for living and leading our most aligned, authentic, and—yes, successful—lives. The activation has begun.

When clients have identified something they really want after an "*aha!*" moment, but don't quite know how to activate next steps, I often hear an audible or inaudible sigh followed by the cliched, "I guess I'll just fake it till I make it."

> Spiritual leadership is both existential and highly practical for living and leading our most aligned, authentic, and successful lives.

I never liked this phrase. It's infested with imposter syndrome. When you call in something that is yours to keep, the last thing you want to do is reinforce a feeling of falsehood. I encourage my clients to lean into the possibility of *acting as if* instead. It's basically a nudge to become this person you are longing for—as if you're already in the middle of it. What would that person say in this situation? How would they act? How might they arrange their day? What types of skills would they learn? With whom would they associate? What would they *not* do?

These open-ended coaching questions allow for manifesting a new reality step by step and day by day. There is nothing *fake* about this. *Act as if* invites you to embody your rediscovered self. So, now, I act as if I'm a modern day medicine woman who is equally passionate about spirituality *and* leadership, authorship *and* taking Emilia to ballet class, profound conversations *and* binge watching Netflix series. Both are true.

The other day, my husband was feeling "off" and he shouted from the other room, "I'm not feeling well."

"Time to do a clearing!" I reassured him.

I shut down my laptop, turned on the space clearing music, centered myself with Archangel Michael, saged our whole space, placed palo santo in the oil diffuser, spoke a silent prayer under my breath, and started pulling oracle cards. I channeled Yiayia in her tiny kitchen across time and space.

I began to yawn.

I share my closeted medicine woman dreams here to show you one of the potential and powerful side effects of the unraveling journey—if you haven't encountered it already. You do the work, you start letting go, you trust a bit more, and you begin to discover lost pieces of yourself. The clues start revealing themselves at a faster clip. You gain momentum and eventually the pieces of this puzzle form a picture that gets clearer and clearer. For some, this might take days, for others, months, or even years. No matter the time continuum (which we now know to trust with reverence as this sacred thing that takes care of us), you are becoming.

As we become the next version of ourselves, we are once again faced with a paradox. How do we let go to face the future while holding onto the sacred past? I have shared so many stories here about my life, my family, my learnings. While unraveling seems to imply a whole lot of letting go, I want to consciously pause here. For every suffocation and fear absorbed through cultural inheritance—especially as a generational first—there is an equally intense and tremendous well of unending love and hope. I know that, were my parents not to face their own unraveling and choose to leave all they knew behind by moving across the world, I would never have the privilege of writing to you. I would never have the confidence to start a business and live a life dedicated to personal leadership, let alone start building a bridge between personal leadership and spiritual leadership. We stand on the shoulders of all those who came before us, and never has this resonated with me as much as it has in the recounting and reliving of these stories. One of my spiritual teachers reassures me that all the healing work we do in this lifetime not only paves the way for the next generation but also heals the generations of the past. I know this sacred unraveling is for me, Emilia, and the mothers, grandmothers, and great-great-great-grandmothers and grandfathers who came before us. This has been not only a journey but a sacred healing quest.

So, did I lose my ambition?

Yes and no. I lost a version of it that was never mine to begin with. The struggle, the angst, the insecurity, the fear, the hustle. Through this journey of unraveling, I discovered a version that was more true—a bit calmer, a bit more at ease, a lot more loving, and a boatload more connected to something larger than myself. The day before writing the conclusion of this book, I had a session with a healer that I've worked with for years. She tuned in and started to share, "Your Angels want you to know that you signed up for this work in this lifetime. Your soul came to heal ancient patterns of struggle that were falsely anchored in conditional love. You chose to live this life as a healer and teacher for expanding the consciousness of love."

I smiled, nodded. Of course I did.

EPILOGUE: HOMECOMING

Writing to you and sharing my story with you, fellow traveler, has been a sincere privilege. As with most stories we feel called to tell, the path certainly wasn't a straight one. I will pause the story here, because what's next is still unwritten—unfolding new insights and lessons each day. Lessons on leadership, entrepreneurship, parenthood, adulthood, marriage, and spirituality.

I really believe that unraveling is a sacred calling, and in spite of the spiritual undertones, also a very practical path towards living a more aligned, joyful, and effortless life. Spiritual leadership as a concept is at its inaugural moment of helping us live more intentional lives while in this earth school—both in our mundane and our meaningful moments. I can't wait to see how our inner spiritual leadership work intersects with our personal and professional lives in the months and years ahead. What a privilege indeed that we get to travel together as we raise our consciousnesses—one thread at a time.

Unraveling exists in the more qualitative and destined *kairos* aspect of time. So, ultimately, it's a bit arbitrary how long the journey actually takes, and it's debatable whether we ever really arrive. Since healing and growth evolve as a spiral rather than a straight line, the journey might take a moment, a few months, or even a lifetime in our linear *chronos* orientation. While my former ambition-driven insides and outsides might find this information frustrating (perhaps even appalling!), my currently much more trusting and perspective-seeking insides sit in wonder of constant evolution during our time here on earth. I believe that when we're truly ready to expand, both the lesson and the teacher synchronistically appear, providing us the opportunities to grow, incredible co-travelers along the way, and clear guideposts that let us know we're on the right path.

> Unraveling is a sacred calling, and in spite of the spiritual undertones, also a very practical path towards living a more aligned, joyful, and effortless life.

If you wander too far in a way that feels off purpose, remember what we've explored here together. The titles of each chapter will help you back onto your unraveling path. Check in with yourself every few months to see where you've made progress and where a deeper dive might be useful. And don't forget the power of story. In our stories lie the secret clues that reveal the rules we live by, the ones that ultimately inform the choices we make, what we value, and the way we orient in the world.

Here's what you can always carry with you as a torch to light your path:

Know the Rules. Always start here. Once you get some clarity on the particular rule that is driving a situation, you have the opportunity to assess whether or not you still want it to drive or whether it's time to direct it to the back seat.

Assess the Bright and Shadow Sides. Every rule and guiding pillar of our life's path has blessings and hindrances. Allow yourself to expand your perspective and look for what is serving you and what is costing you so you have all the (subjective) facts. (Another paradox!)

Rekindle Your Strengths. Our strengths are the divine gems hidden within us to uncover and leverage throughout this lifetime. Ensure that you make visible what is uniquely yours and invest time and energy in leading from this place. This is where flow lives.

Get Curious. Curiosity eats judgment for breakfast and judgment might be the most obvious way that fear and insecurity show up in our lives. Allow yourself to ask bold questions (e.g. "What do I need to learn here?") to help unlock any situation.

Get Courageous. Courage lives in the tiny moments of our lives, not necessarily the grand gestures. Consider how you orient yourself to what you really want and ensure that you are committing to one or two brave moments each day.

Stay on Your Own Journey. Looking over your shoulders to assess, fix, or intervene in someone else's journeys disrupts your moment *and* robs the other co-traveler of their own insights and growth. Keep your emotional boundaries up for the good of all.

Speak Your Truth. Putting language and daily practices into who you really are versus who you think you *should* be unlocks the alignment between your insides and your outsides. Allow yourself to speak (and listen!) to what matters most to you.

Love (as a Verb). Love is the greatest force in the universe. In actively practicing love, you begin to harness this limitless power into new ways of thinking, feeling, and engaging with your challenges and opportunities.

Allow the Paradox. Giving permission to your mind and heart to sit with two seemingly disparate things at once expands your ability to lead through change and navigate the inevitable chaos of being human. Allow the paradox to inspire you.

Act as If. Once you've discovered enough clues, don't wait to live the life you intend. There is no magical time or space where you officially arrive. Act as if you are already there and watch the wonder of the universe transpiring for your good.

Homecoming. Each step of your unraveling journey is one step closer to coming home. A home that you have created—inspired by your past, anchored in your present, and intentioned for your future. Welcome home.

• • •

My husband and I make it a point to pick Emilia up from nursery school together whenever we can. She is usually immersed in play, glances over at us when we call, and runs into our arms as if she's seeing us for the first time. It's our simplest and most divine pleasure of the day. On our way out of her classroom the other day, I noticed a poster that had photos of several children playing in the mud puddles after the bizarrely wet California winter. She was up front and center in one of the photos, looking like she owned the damn mud puddle, and I rejoiced, "Emilia—look—it's you!"

She looked up at the photo, sighed, and said nonchalantly, "I love me."

Kosta and I both laughed out loud, but as we looked straight at each other, I knew there was something deeper we were communicating beyond words. All the work we have done on unraveling our collective challenges with self-esteem, self-love, courage, confidence, trust were reflected back in that singular moment. All of our "I'm not enough" years were instantly replaced with her "I love myself" declaration and knowingness. Our unraveling was worth every excruciating and provocative minute—we're writing our future from the present rather than from the past—all while healing both the generation ahead and the ones that came before.

> Each step we take towards unraveling yet another thread of our journey is the same exact step towards becoming who we intend to be.

This is where I leave you—for now. Notice that I could have replaced the word *unraveling* with *becoming* throughout this book. Each step we take towards unraveling yet another thread of our journey is the same exact step towards becoming who we intend to be. Welcome to the paradox of leadership.

POSTSCRIPT: DRAFT OF POTENTIAL NEW RULES

Still a work in progress, fellow travelers. Here are some of the new rules I'm considering and hoping to pass onto Emilia.

Start with love. Above all else, you are seen, you belong, you are adored—love yourself each day.

Stay in wonder. The world is full of the same wonder that you are made of—follow the wonder clues.

Lead with strengths. Your purpose lies in your naturally embedded strengths—the Divine put them there for you to discover and use.

Learn to pivot. Forgive yourself and others early and often—grace will take care of the rest.

Align with the Divine. Trust in change and have faith in the changeless—you are safe no matter what.

SHARE THE LOVE (AS A VERB).

> "Buy this book for yourself and devour it as I did. You'll never stop thanking yourself. Then buy this book for everyone you know. You'll be making the world a better place."
>
> - Kate Vanek, Global COO & CFO, *True Platform*

Hello again! It's Valia.

I'm so grateful you've stuck with me until the very end. I hope you've found the courage to embark on your own unraveling journey. It has been my honor to travel with you, and I trust we will meet again. If you've found this book inspiring and helpful, please share it generously! My mission is to support as many humans as possible while they align their insides with their outsides.

Here are a few ways you can support me and the work:

- Share the book as a gift with those who matter most to you: www.unravelingambition.com! Special bulk discounts are available if you would like your whole team or organization to benefit from reading this. I'm happy to provide you with material in running a book club, an organization-wide event, or teaching an in-house course. Contact me at valia@leadwithvalia.com.
- Consider leaving a review wherever you bought the book. Online bookstores are more likely to promote a book when they feel good about its content, and reader reviews are the best barometer for a book's quality. I know this takes a few extra minutes of time, but it goes a long way.
- Lastly, I take a limited number of speaking and leadership development engagements each year and would be delighted to support you and your organization as you move towards more purposeful and intentional leadership. Email me directly at valia@leadwithvalia.com so we can find some time to discuss.

Thank you for being an integral part of spreading the word about *Unraveling Ambition* and its leadership messages. I am humbled and grateful.

With love,
Valia

ABOUT THE AUTHOR

 As a highly sought-after trainer, facilitator, coach and speaker, Valia Glytsis is known for her inspirational and transformative approach to leadership development—leading from the inside-out. Valia is proud to call leadership development her ministry. She is the CEO and Founder of *The Paradox of Leadership*, a boutique learning and development firm serving senior executives and their leadership teams to deepen trust, cultivate communication, and build alignment. She is fascinated by the space where business and spirituality meet and has made it her mission to invite other progressive leaders into this exploration.

Her authorship debut, *Unraveling Ambition*, is a testament to her passion for helping clients rewrite their stories and unlock more meaning and purpose in how they live and lead.

Originally from New York, she and her husband Kostas chased the sun to Newport Beach, California. They both work tirelessly for their bosses: a toddler named Emilia and a Boston Terrier named Henry.

To learn more about Valia: www.leadwithvalia.com
To learn more about The Paradox of Leadership:
www.theparadoxofleadership.com